The Common Sense of Teaching Foreign Languages

Caleb Gattegno

Educational Solutions Worldwide Inc.

First published in 1976. Reprinted in 2010.

Copyright © 1976-2010 Educational Solutions Worldwide Inc.
Author: Caleb Gattegno
All rights reserved
ISBN 978-0-87825-231-2

Educational Solutions Worldwide Inc.
2nd Floor 99 University Place, New York, N.Y. 10003-4555
www.EducationalSolutions.com

Acknowledgments

The manuscript of this book has been read by a number of friends whose suggestions were almost always found to be an improvement on the original.

A suggestion which I could not incorporate in the text was to make the text easy to read. My style, developed originally when writing mathematics papers, is found by many to be demanding. Perhaps this is because I write concisely and I avoid developments that readers feel they need but that do not suggest themselves to me.

One of my advisers found it useful to read aloud every sentence that seemed too dense, and clarity sometimes resulted. Perhaps I will be permitted to pass on this tip to my readers.

I want to thank Zulette Catir and Bill Bernhardt for their linguistic help and Clermonde Dominicé for preparing the book for the printers, Cecilia Bartoli, Clermonde again, Shiow Ley Kuo and Patricia Perez for their contributions in exploiting on behalf of some of our readers the word charts of Italian, French, Mandarin and Spanish. These form the appendices connected with my Chapter 7 which was written with the English charts as my guide.

Table of Contents

Preface 1

1 Freeing the Students 7

2 The Most Basic Component 23

3 The Next Step 37

4 Perception 43

5 Independence, Autonomy and Responsibility 57

6 Uses of Rods and Charts 69

    A. Examples of Introducing Triggers for: 79
        1. A Cluster of Expressions in Space Relations 79
        2. A Cluster of Expressions in Temporal Relations 80
        3. Some Causes and Effects 80

    B. Making Subtle Distinctions Visible: 81
        1. While, At the Same Time, Simultaneously, During 81
        2. Because, For, As, Though, Since, Before, Already, Then 82
        3. If, Whether, Supposing 84

    C. Extending to Life Experiences. 84

  1. A Clock 84
  2. The Calendar 86
  3. Today, Yesterday, Tomorrow, etc. 87
  4. Various Plans of Houses, Schools, Hospitals, etc. 89

7 Exploiting the Functional Vocabulary 93

 A. Sentences 101
  Chart 1 101
  Charts 1 & 2 102

 B. Sentences 102
  Chart 1 102
  Charts 1 & 2 103

 C. Sentences 104
  Chart 1 104
  Charts 1, 2, 3 105
  Charts 1-4 106
  Charts 1-5 106
  Charts 1-6 107
  Charts 1-7 107
  Charts 1-8 108
  Charts 1-9 109
  Charts 1-10 109
  Charts 1-11 110
  Charts 1-12 110

8 Reading and Writing in the New Language 113

9 Expansion of Vocabulary...121

Treatment of one of the Pictures as an Example:
The Family. 135
A Thousand Sentences. 138

10 Evaluating Progress... 145

11 Short Passages And Stories 165

Short Passages. 166
Mark And Teresa 170

Appendices 181

French 181
    Tableaux 1.. 181
    Tableaux 1 et 2..182
    Tableaux 1, 2 et 3..183
    Tableaux 1-4 184
    Tableaux 1-5 186
    Tableaux 1-6 187
    Tableaux 1-7 188
    Tableaux 1-8 189
    Tableaux 1-9 190
    Tableaux 1-10 191
    Tableaux 1-11 192

Italian 194
    Tabella 1..194

  Tabelle 1 & 2 195
  Tabelle 1, 2 & 3 196
  Tabelle 1-4 197
  Tabelle 1-5 298
  Tabelle 1-6 200
  Tabelle 1-7 201
  Tabelle 1-8 203
  Tabelle 1-9 204
  Tabelle 1-10 206
  Tabelle 1-11 207
  Tabelle 1-12 209
 Spanish 211
  Làmina 1 211
  Làminas 1 Y 2 212
  Làminas 1, 2 Y 3 214
  Làminas 1-4 215
  Làminas 1-5 216
  Làminas 1-6 218
  Làminas 1-7 220
  Làminas 1-8 221
  Làminas 1-9 223
  Làminas 1-10 224
  Làminas 1-12 226
 Mandarin 228

Bibliography 241

Preface

A slim book written in 1962, published in England in 1963 and reprinted with only stylistic changes in the United States in 1972 is all the public has had to look at about the approach, now known as "The Silent Way," which I started to develop in April 1954 and am still working on. This book is both a summary of what I have learned over these years and the latest statement on the subject I can make as a scientist examining the whole area of language learning and teaching.

In my previous book I told a number of the investigations I had to carry out in order to understand the field and be able to work in it. Some of these were of intrinsic interest (such as how babies learn to speak their mother tongue) and have been included in subsequent monographs which do not refer to the study of foreign languages. Some had not been sufficiently examined at the time to yield a conclusion one way or another. For example, I felt then that I could write a teachers' guide but soon found that not one but many needed to be written, a challenge my life could not accommodate. In the 1972 reprint of the work, references to teachers' guides were deleted. In the present book it will be seen how a great deal more can be said to language teachers that usually belongs to teachers' guides, without having to write a book for each language in each of the languages teachers use for their study.

A number of the chapters in this book summarize years of field work which took me to a number of countries to meet teachers and their needs as best I could in the opportunities offered by my visits, some of which were repeated, some prolonged. Occasionally I worked on the production of materials on my own and submitted the results of that work to select individuals who were native speakers of the languages in question. What I had to do with myself to be able to tackle a new language is known only to me, but the result of my work had to be tested with students to insure that indeed some of the difficult challenges of each language could be met by the learners competently and, hence, confidently. These tests replaced the usual submission to native speakers' views on how to teach their language. In fact very rarely have I met a native who was as sensitive to his or her language as I needed to be in order to help foreigners conquer it in a reasonably short time through classroom work. On the whole natives are not the best source for the solutions of the challenge since their own language is as functional for them as their digestion—which rarely becomes the object of their attention.

I speak here with two voices: with one as a student of languages because I wish to feel myself inching towards what natives do with themselves when they use their language spontaneously for expression in all occasions; with the other as a teacher, because I want to do the "right" things for my students. Once I understand what students have to do, I am able to invent techniques and materials that help them to be as good as the natives in what they are facing.

Because of this insight into the connection between teaching and learning, it has been possible to use teaching as a way of investigating what learning is while it takes place and through it to affect teaching, and so on.

Some obvious notions have been hidden from our sight, mainly because we were engaged in "doing our own thing."

- We are retaining systems and do not need to stress memorization as much as most teachers do. We hold better in our minds what we meet with awareness.

- Students must relate to the new language and practice it to make it their own; to relate to anything else is a distraction and distractions interfere with learning.

- Teachers must be concerned with what the students are doing with themselves rather than with the language, which is the students' concern. Teachers and students work on different subjects.

- The ability to repeat immediately what a speaker has uttered is no proof of retention.

- Hearing something said several times does not guarantee retention, still less understanding, of it.

- Not all learning takes place here and now; some may well be the outcome of sleeping on it.

- It is possible to notice differences between what one says or thinks and what others say or think, but only when one works on oneself do changes happen. So we must make students work on themselves as a matter of course.

- Since all learning is in time and is progressive, we need not request perfection (which in any case is unattainable) but only be concerned with steady improvement.

- We can also be concerned with as good an achievement as can be reached all the time, leading to the best results cumulatively.

- If at every moment learning has taken place, then it is clear that the integration of every day's contribution makes it possible for students to function better all the time.

- Since we are concerned with human beings studying a language, we are concerned with awareness and not with the accumulation of knowledge; with facility, and not erudition. Awareness demands of the teachers that they know what to do at every moment, facility demands of the students that they give themselves to the tasks and practice them *per se*. It is the students' need for facility that imposes silence upon the teacher.

Preface

We have qualified all these points as obvious on reflection, and we learn from our inability to see them at once as such that we set our sight on some other matters. This book may contribute to reset our sight on such points and make them play their part in our enlightenment.

Caleb Gattegno
New York City
May 1976

1 Freeing the Students

The experience we all have in using our own language for the expression of our thoughts, feelings, emotions, and perceptions is that words come by themselves, that we have at our disposal an extremely effective automatic system which demands almost no energy to function. Under such conditions, language is truly a vehicle; it carries our expressions to our satisfaction.

As soon as we leave our own language and concentrate on acquiring a new one, however, we find that we are engaged in struggles, that our memory becomes so important, whereas in our own language it does not seem to play a big role. In fact we can no more say that we 'remember' our language than that we remember how to stand up or walk. We know how to speak. We feel that knowing a language is a skill, not the memorization of statements, that it is ours as a functioning. So much so that, in our conversations with our relatives and friends, we never attempt to retain the words we use and hear, once the meaning has been either expressed or understood.

As students and teachers we are confronted with the contrast of something that looks as obvious to the latter as it does strange to the former. All the efforts of teachers have tended towards making the gap between themselves and their students disappear, though this attempt is rarely successful. If students manage to learn by doing the right things with themselves, teachers can find support in their success for what they have been attempting. But it would seem fairer to assess our approaches by concentrating upon those who do not succeed and to develop an evaluation of our proposal based on the number of people who manage, at a "reasonable" cost in time and effort, to feel that they are advancing towards expressing themselves like natives of the new language. If we can reach almost all who turn to us to acquire a language, we can say with confidence that we know what we are doing. If, on the contrary, we gather evidence that we lose many students, or that after years at it they can not show much for their efforts, we can ask ourselves if our approach is at fault.

Since we know the state of feeling free of the demands of a language when we use it fluently to express ourselves, it is appropriate for teachers to ask: "When can we say that we are freeing our students?" and to spend more time examining the answer to this question.

Freeing our students means giving them in the new language the know-how they already possess in their mother tongue.

In speaking the mother tongue no energy is spent in controlling the sounds uttered. They come by themselves, align themselves one after the other to form the words of our language, the right words with the right stresses, in the right order. The voice supplies the intonation, and the melody, which in turn convey much of the meaning.

No energy is spent in letting words trigger images and images trigger words. Images generate what is called the meaning of words. As to the words themselves, their criterion of acceptability is their *consistency* with 1) that exchange between the source of truth, extracted from reality by so many mental processes and residing in our acceptance of our images, and 2) the conventional organization of the words. That words do not convey meaning by themselves is at once clear if one switches to listening to a language one does not know. Words are arbitrary, but they are also consistent, and it is the perception of consistency that offers a basis to our mind for the retention we already managed as babies. There is truth in perception and in feeling, and in our perception of our feelings. We need truth to be free and we recognize truth as soon as we meet it at the level of perception and feeling.

We now know that if we use the light of remaining in contact with truth, we shall be better equipped in our study of how to free our students, who have no basis for a belief that they can cope with the demands of the enormous expansion of the unknown which a new language represents in the beginning and continues to represent for some time.

The truth that the utterances must be consciously constructed by each of our students is a precious guide. It will dictate how we must work with our students and which materials and techniques we must develop in order to reach as soon as possible that level of functioning which will take care of the next movement towards another of the obstacles in their way.

The truth that meaning is conveyed by perception will give words a chance to become triggers in the new language, just as they are in the old one. This truth will also dictate which materials and techniques are best for the presentation of the fabric of languages, their grammar. In fact, remaining in contact with this truth will establish the fact that mastery is not achieved at the end of a course but everyday and on a precise, definite matter. Then everyday, about each of these matters, the teacher can say to the students: "And now, on this you are as good as I am."

But these daily conquests do not remain isolated events: through the cumulative effect of learning they are subsumed under an integrated mastery which covers more and more of the language. Our students will be free of anxiety if they can sense *a)* that they are not required to do more than is being done and, in particular, are not left to think that the whole language must be at their disposal when only a little has been explored and *b)* that what they have done has been done well, occupies their time, and gives them the impression that they are on top of things, possessing criteria and a sense of thoroughness.

For the first, it may be necessary to tell them, in their vernacular, that we have accepted our responsibility as teachers to make them users of the language presented, even good users, and that we shall accept what they produce and work on it, never asking for what does not seem possible to the students, never forgetting that they are beginners, learners, explorers of the unknown.

For the second, we must know precisely what to do all the time. This is a technical matter which cannot be met by bright ideas unless we are very lucky. Looking at all the proposals for teaching foreign languages that have had large numbers of followers, we can easily find that they provided no basis for a belief that they could free students and, therefore, succeed in making all students into competent learners.

Each of us is equipped with a facility to utter what we hear. Hence we should not be surprised that students can easily repeat but not retain what a native speaker says. The exercise of repetition only tells us that we are equipped to repeat, not that repetition is our way of learning a language. Babies show us that they do not use repetition for a good two or three years. Every baby is aware that he must consciously utter what he wills, and only then does he listen to it and use what he knows as an utterer and hearer to identify what is being said by others.

No baby by-passes the conscious stage of knowing what sounds to make, but the audio-lingual approaches deliberately fall into the trap of using drill and repetition as a way of bringing the new language to their students.

Translation is a method of conveying the meaning of utterances in the new languages when these meanings already exist in the mind of the learners in association with words of their native language. But clearly, as in the mother tongue, once the meaning has been reached the word can be dropped. How then could a student know how to produce the new language if the meaning only triggers his mother tongue? Those of us who have studied one or more languages via translation know that, rather than feeling free in the new language, we felt paralyzed.

This does not mean that there is no place in life for translation. It is an easy task whenever we know two languages well, at least in the areas where we can shift from words in one language to the meanings they refer to and then to words in the second language and conversely. The words which trigger meanings must do so in conformity with an area of experience in which the translator has access to truth. How many can cite examples of natives being as lost in front of a text in their own language as the foreigner who turns to them for help?

Translation is not a way of freeing students; it is the job of specialists. Drill and repetition do not serve the purpose any better.

Although there are people who have managed to conquer a language through either of these approaches, the analysis of the evidence tells us that, as far as freeing the majority of students is concerned, they cannot claim to be successful.

What then is left to consider?

We can become sensitive to the problems of learning a language. We can establish what students bring of themselves to their new language that can serve as a basis to an approach that has a chance of culminating with people functioning in the new language as they do in their own, i.e., free to express what they want in the manner that is as close to meaning as they can find in their own language.

All students who are not babies or are not handicapped know what a language is for and how to handle their flow of words as a functioning; we do not have to teach them that.

All students know—even if not in too sharp a manner—that, while listening requires the cooperation of their self, what they hear is what other people put into the air. To speak, on the contrary, requires the descent of the will into the voluntary speech organs and a clear grasp by one's linguistic self of what there is to do to produce definite sounds in definite ways. Only the self of the utterer can intervene to make objective what it holds in itself. Every student must be seen as a will capable of that work.

Moreover, since very early or in infancy every one of us noticed that careful listening is necessary to know what we hear and that we have the power to act on the speech organs to produce utterances having certain properties, every student can be granted the power of self-correction, of conscious correction.

Perhaps this is the place to distinguish "granting" from "taking for granted." In the perspective of studying learning and teaching knowingly, we must refrain from taking anything for granted but must also at the same time grant students every one of the components of learning for which there is evidence. For example, we must not take for granted that what we think is known to others and that our hopes and expectations are justified. But if students have learned at least one language we must grant them that they have learned something akin to what we are now presenting to them, however different the two languages may be.

This point could be a test for our readers, who are invited to watch whether this writer observes the distinction between granting and taking for granted in what follows. If self-correction is required in any case, whether the teacher acts as a model or not, it seems sensible to use it deliberately. Self-correction assumes self-awareness, and it is awareness that is educable, i.e., can be brought to realization of what needs to be done, what changes in functioning are required. Awareness mobilizes the will. Each student brings with him his capacity of becoming aware of his functionings and proves this be correcting himself.

Each student is a learning system and has proved so several times over in his life. We can grant him that, when confronting the new language, he will act again as a learning system, i.e., will mobilize what is required by the tasks from his arsenal of achievements and from that part of his potential called in by the challenges.

Every student is a retaining system; this means that the impacts on each of them leave a track that can be recalled without any special gift being assumed. The power to produce images for what we see or hear, feel or smell, is brought by us to all the circumstances of life, and we can grant this power to our students. In particular, we do not have to teach our language students concepts which have already been formed by their retaining self in the acquisition of their native language. But we have to distinguish what makes sense by itself, for which recall is immediate, from what is arbitrary and not necessary. For example, a mistake native speakers of English often make, when taught to read by a whole word approach, is to say "boat" when shown the word "ship," or conversely. This mistake tells us that "ship" and "boat" by the criteria of association in the spoken language may trigger the same images, and, therefore, may be considered as equivalent. In order for only one utterance for the written word to be retained, the association must be prevented and the unique sound associated with the shape of the word must be deliberately connected.

To speak more precisely of these matters, I have introduced the word "ogden" to refer to the mobilization of mental energy required to link permanently (i.e., for long durations and at the beck and call of one's will) two mental elements, such as a sound and a shape, a shape or a sound and a meaning, a label and an object, etc.

"Ogdens" are not needed for functionings, such as perception, or for recognition of emotions or images, but they are required every time we wish to commit to memory those items that are arbitrary. In the field of language the retention of 10,000 words may require the expenditure of 10,000 ogdens.

Hence, if we want to free our students, we must make sure that they actually spend the ogdens when they need to be spent. Sometimes a mere request for re-iteration of the question shows that students have not forgotten and proves that an ogden has in fact been paid.

Triggers of response do not always require the entire original expenditure of energy because recognition, as a power of the mind, enables us to use a limited amount of information to complete a message. For instance, "m—th—r" is sufficient to trigger the whole word "mother."

To grant our students the use of their powers of recognition will help both them and their teacher in presenting them with material that can yield a great deal more than the expenditure of ogdens alone permits.

For instance, equivalent expressions, so prevalent in the use of language, serve us well when our memory fails. We would not feel free to use our language for our own ends if we were not equipped to replace a word by a circumlocution, or one statement by several others. Ogdens are not involved in equivalent expressions. In fact the purpose of the equivalence is to make good with what one has retained in place of what one cannot recall at that moment. It is a sign of the self's intimate knowledge of its memory and its weaknesses, and we should be sensitive to it when we teach by not relying too much on memory.

Our students' *intelligence* is another power they bring with them. The role of intelligence is to supply other powers of the self when one is confronted with challenges that resist the attack they initially suggested. Thus intelligence tells students that they function better when relaxed than when tense and invites them to consent to enter exercises which reduce anxiety. It also tells them that association helps retention and that rote memorization is useless. In particular, it shows them that it is easier to group words, in order to distinguish or assimilate them, and to learn clusters than to memorize isolated items.

Intelligence advises us to use all available means to conquer the content of a situation and to make use of what everyone else in the class can contribute to the tasks at hand *rather* than to compete with everyone.

Intelligence is not a luxury; its functions are vital and basic and can do much to increase students' feeling that learning a language is an exciting adventure involving the whole self. All through our lessons it will shine by being given a central presence.

Our students also bring *imagination* to our classes. Once we have learned to have it as part of our work with them, we need not postpone its use until much later in our courses when composition is considered. From very early on and throughout, we can call upon imagination to widen students' involvement with the materials, so that these lose their apparent limitations.

We can therefore say that we are freeing our students when:

- we do not take anything for granted;

- we grant our students all they bring with them that is relevant to language learning, in particular, that we recognize that they are

    1. learning systems motivated by learning itself,

    2. retaining systems every time they function,

    3. intelligent persons,

    4. imaginative persons,

    5. persons capable of thinking in equivalences, and

    6. persons aware of the weaknesses of rote memorization and aware of the powers of recognition and of association,

    7. persons capable of distinguishing components in their experience and of correcting themselves once they form their own criteria,

    8. persons having a will which can be called on all the time to act or to stop themselves from acting,

    9. persons capable of suspending judgment until evidence is available to make one take some steps,

    10. persons capable of relating to truth and of preventing the interference of preconceptions and distractions,

11 persons who can at every moment judge whether they are using themselves properly or wasting their time,

12 persons capable of seeing that much can be done with a little, a functional little, but in which they must invest by paying the required ogdens,

13 persons capable of seeing that much can be inferred, deduced, generalized, combined, extended and, thus, persons capable of extending their time far beyond the hours of direct involvement in the learning.

The last point brings us to the contribution of sleep in making each of us into a more effective learner.

Sleep indeed is for learning, for sorting out—in terms of energy—whether what we went through in our waking state was endowed with too much or too little energy, whether the suspected links have been followed through, whether associations need to be made, etc.

If we have found in our own life that sleep helps us in our learning, we shall be able to free our students from the absurd burden of trying to be perfect here and now. We shall only induce them to work out in their sleep a number of the difficult exercises required of our soma by the new language which escape our waking consciousness. Indeed, in sleep we can avoid the pressures of the outside world and be true to ourselves and our endowments. This phenomenon makes available gifts related to our early childhood and, because of this, leads us to be much better in our performances after sleep than before.

When we take up in detail in the appropriate chapters the technical aspects of all these findings which result from our use of common sense, we shall find, on the one hand, that our approach is not a mosaic of bright ideas but a solid arrangement of necessary actions and, on the other hand, that we can consider the challenge of teaching language to be reduced to a scientific study of the field in which the students as persons are at least as important as the language.

In fact, we can see that teachers and students have two very different functions. The latter are dedicated to acquiring a language, and they must feel that they are in fact exchanging their time for that acquisition. The former do not have to work on the language while teaching, but only on the students: on what they are doing or not doing, on their progress towards mastery of every item being worked on, and on offering them exercises or suggestions that lead to the required mastery.

Language teaching becomes a scientific endeavor because the teacher is engaged in what makes things move in the proper direction knowingly and carefully through access to a continuous feedback of what students are doing here and now.

For these reasons, teachers of language can stop being record players, can be mostly silent, and can delegate the responsibility of learning to the learners in a manner that shows them also as responsible for what their part is. No congratulation or criticism is needed, for all is matter of fact. The subordination of teaching to learning is the only way of handling the challenge of freeing students while ensuring that they learn by an economic exchange of their time for a maximum learning.

Such learning is not forgotten simply because no one has been asked to remember anything. Retention, being a functioning of the self, will take place as a matter of course, and students, who all are linguists, will end up owning a language as they own other skills.

2 The Most Basic Component

Is it not common sense in language learning and teaching to treat as basic the one component found in all circumstances where language is used? Especially if it is as pervasive as is the emission of the sounds of a language?

Every time we open our mouths for expression, we make use of our utterances. These utterances precede both the formation of sentences, hence the appearance of structures, and the adequacy to meaning, hence the vocabulary. Since these two aspects of language need the sounds of a language to be objectified, they will be better founded if the sounds are first well established. From the perspective of freeing the students, moreover, it is obvious that a neglect of the basic foundation leads from a shaky contact with the language in the beginning to a continuing uncertainty into the future.

In fact, we all meet students of language who, after years of studying grammar and vocabulary, of reading papers, magazines and books, are uncertain of some of the most common words in that language and appear weaker than their gifts should allow them to be.

For years we have been working with the awareness that students must become independent, autonomous, and responsible in the field of sound production. The results of this work have taken several forms, each one showing a concern for doing the job with whatever materials were then available.

In 1962, when the first Silent Way classroom materials were printed for English, French, and Spanish, the fact that we used the same colors whenever the sounds of the languages were close enough provided the basis for indicating immediately to students that, if they knew how to produce sounds in one of the languages, they could produce them for the other two as well. Moreover, they could also find where they should concentrate in order to complete their acquaintance with *all* the sounds of the language being studied.

This classroom material consists of word charts, which are made to hang on a wall and which display the intended sounds by means of a color code. Students who are able to read a few of the words can use these as references to decode other words on their own. To that extent they have been made independent. They become autonomous if they can take the initiative to find out how many of the words they can crack at each stage of their exposure to the charts. They become responsible to the extent that they can systematically and carefully use what has been made available to them through the coloring.

In addition, we have produced for each language a chart that we have dubbed the *Fidel* (an Ethiopian word borrowed in 1957 in the first attempt at organizing the sounds and spelling of a language). We have a score of these at present, and their contribution to language teaching has grown with their number. (A comparative kit is being contemplated and is, in fact, in the process of being produced. It will allow students whose language is included in the kit to have an independent entry into the sounds and the script of nineteen other languages.)

The Fidels are much more useful teaching tools now than when they were created. Originally, they served to display both the totality of sounds of a language and the totality of spellings accorded in each language to those sounds. They presented visually the extent of what students had to know in order to be at peace with their utterances and their writing. But to really own these two aspects of a language students had to relate to some content, and for this a teacher acquainted with the materials was needed. This is less the case today because the comparative kit is, in part, available.

Each Fidel is divided into two parts: the upper part containing signs for the vowels in the shapes provided by the script of the language—except in the case of Chinese where we have used colored rectangles; the lower part (set off by a horizontal line) containing the signs for consonants, which, however, cannot be sounded alone.

A pointer is used to form words on the Fidel by touching swiftly a sequence of selected signs to indicate the order of merged utterances that make a word. The explicit objectivity of this activity confers a truth to each word, and, if students know how to produce the sounds associated with the colors, they may in the end produce a word in the new language.

When it is possible to place two Fidels side by side, one of the native language of the students and one of the new language, the teacher can be totally silent for all the sounds shared by the two languages. Otherwise, an utterance by the teacher may suffice to put the new sound into circulation.

The responsibility of the teacher is discharged when the sound is produced loudly and clearly, before the attentive audience.

The students come equipped to receive sounds and to transfer through their brain, the characteristics that make such sounds capable of being uttered voluntarily. Someone usually proves that this transfer of sound heard into sound uttered is easy. Most of the rest of the class can acknowledge the naturalness of such transfer while the teacher concentrates on those who find it harder and directs them to listen to those who succeed.

Various languages have developed unique, idiosyncratic features which from the beginning must be made conscious to the student. For instance, Spanish vowels keep their value anywhere in the word: they are called pure. But this is not the case for English, German, Russian, etc. English has non-descript vowels for most unstressed syllables, and no word will sound like English until these are produced spontaneously be the speakers.

Vowels are the most important element to work on in the beginning, and we have found that, if they are done well, students are helped immensely in all that follows.

It is always possible to form "words" using only vowels by pointing at them in certain orders—even if such words do not exist in the language. These vowel sequences can be uttered carefully, as the students understand exactly the meaning of the game of pointing, and, if these are well chosen, students will be producing a number of parts of words that will be met in the vocabulary of the new language.

In Spanish for example: *oí* is a word; *oía* another; *ee, eo* and *eia* are needed in such verbs as *lee, leo, veo, leía, veía,* and others.

Also in Spanish, by considering that the mute letter *h* only produces alternative spellings for the vowel sounds, we make available at once a number of useful words: *ha, he, hay, hoy* (and *ya, yo* by reversing the last two sounds, and *ay,* as another word).

Each language suggests a specific use of its Fidel. We shall illustrate our contribution in this field using two of them. Had we used a different pair, the actual results would have been utterly different in appearance. Still we can learn much that is valid for most languages, provided we adapt the approach to the particular demands of each one. I have on some occasions used the Fidel of one language to produce sentences in another language. For instance, using the Amharic Fidel, we can make quite a number of statements which sound like French sentences and trigger their meaning as French although they are nonsensical in Amharic.

The following are reproductions of the Spanish Fidel for the dialect of some parts of South America and the Japanese Fidel for the Hiragana alphabet. The vowel sounds represented are the same in both, and the order can be deduced from one if the other is known. The convention that signs in the same column correspond to the same sound applies to vowels in both cases and to consonants in Spanish. For Japanese the signs below the horizontal line represent syllables, except in the last column on the right, which refers to three consonants. The colors have not been reproduced here and readers will have to use their imagination.

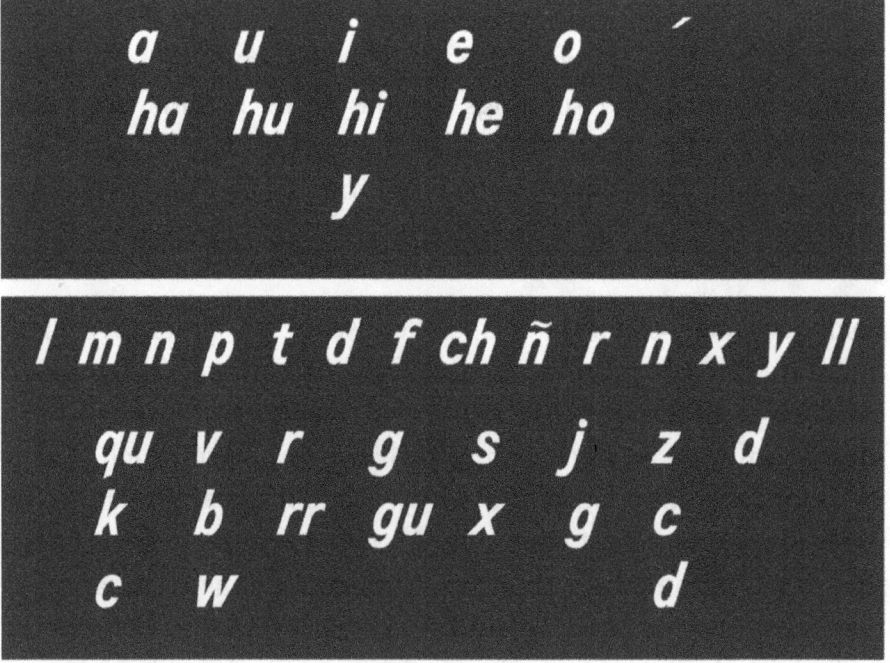

2 The Most Basic Component

っ
お え う い あ
お え う い あ
を へ う い あ

ん ろ れ る り ら
ん の ね ぬ に な
　 も め む み ま
　 ほ へ ふ ひ は
　 ぼ べ ぶ び ば
　 ぽ ぺ ぷ ぴ ぱ
　 と て つ ち た
　 ど で づ ぢ だ
　 よ 　 ゆ 　 や
　 こ け く き か
　 ご げ ぐ ぎ が
　 そ せ す し さ
ん ぞ ぜ ず じ ざ
　 は 　 　 　 わ

Because there are four components to attend to when proposing the exercises with pointers on the Fidel, we must introduce the gestures for indicating the stress in words, the "running on" of words in phrases, and the demands on one's voice to produce the intonation and the melody of each language.

The place of stress in words of more than one syllable can be shown in two ways: 1) on the Fidel by touching a particular vowel sign more forcefully with the pointer, 2) by showing the students a virtual placing of syllables on segments of one index finger as if the word were unrolled, e.g.: a—mi—go would use three segments: one for *a,* one for *mi,* one for *go,* and lifting the finger on the pointer that is sweeping the index carrying the word when *mi* is pointed at. Shapes like

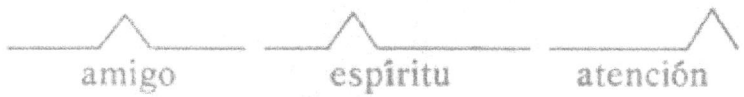

illustrate this procedure.

For phrasing we use several fingers of one or more hands (with one finger representing one word), separating them if a short pause exists, holding them together if they run on together. For instance, *"Mi amigo no está en su casa."* yields a 2-2-3 grouping of words while *"Y en aquél lugar no hay nada."* yields a 4-3 "melody," as we call it.

Using his hands as a conductor, a teacher calls for either a uniform level of sound production demanded by, say, the Japanese language, or a raising or lowering of voice as asked for by Spanish. In a number of languages this gives a physiognomy to each sentence, and this alone can serve as a booster to newcomers to a language.

It must be clear here that we are not concerned with the meaning implied in any sentence. The meaning we are concerned with is of the rules of the game which is being described. Students are going to use themselves to respond to some pointings, some stresses, to running on and melody. If they observe the rules, what they utter may make total sense to natives and none at all to them.

Before using this approach teachers must be at peace with this demand, one which some find inadmissible. Students of whatever age play it comfortably and say they enjoy it. For our purpose of increasing the yield in language learning, it is a very important contribution since it will tackle once and for all the component which will be used all the time and it will free students from its pervading demand on them. In fact the whole outcome of these exercises seems unbelievable. In their first hour of entering a new language, students who are not offered a model to guide them end up uttering with remarkable ease and fluency sentences formed of thirty words, or so, that no native can conceive as not being understood by the utterers. This is so because they are not repeating what a native has said; which normally in his case would be associated with meaning.

What must be understood at this moment is that a teacher using this approach has access to the powers of the students: i.e., the power to look and interpret what is being seen in terms of accepted conventions practiced here and now, the power to utter what one's intelligence has reached, and the power to mold the utterances to accommodate stress, phrasing, and melody according to the demands of the teacher through agreed conventions. Because the connections between signs and sounds exist, in opposite order for the teacher than for the student, the result of the utterances by the students is one or more sentences that the teacher would have uttered for the meaning he started with, only he has pointed at signs on a Fidel and the students have uttered the outcome on his behalf.

Forming words at first by pointing and seeing to it that the sounds are those agreed upon but saying nothing, the teacher can make selections, using the vowels with either one consonant or as many consonants as are easily utterable by the students.

Here are a few examples in Spanish, using *l* alone for the first case: *"lía lee—lilí le leía—lola lo leía—a él lulú lee—lola olía el alelí."*

And for the second: *"no hay—hoy no hay nada—ni él ni su mamá están comiendo—cuando salieron de la casa ella tenía en su mano su paraguas mientras él llevaba un abrigo."*

It is just as easy to make sentences in Japanese, but the composition of the characters will preclude doing so here. With a pointer we can elicit after one hour of exposure of the kind described above utterances which sound like this: *"momo ilo no bo, o ippon to kiloibo o nihon totte kudasai."* The great booster found in this exercise is in the intimate knowledge that one can produce a longish statement fluently without ever having heard it, that one's intelligence has been used to enlist the various sensitivities present in oneself in order to solve a specific problem at the level of sound production, that all distractions have been eliminated and that one has concentrated exclusively on the tasks at hand.

Because the challenges are real for the students, they find themselves motivated to enter them and to keep on playing the games. Because there is no waste of energy and each new step is truly new, either integrating what has been done earlier and producing longer statements, or expanding what already seemed a feat a minute earlier, or referring to utterances of a few minutes ago now used with new ones in addition, students find themselves recognizing the exercises in which they become involved as true games similar to the many they have used successfully in their prior apprenticeships.

Because there is no demand that anyone remember anything but only the activity of letting the lean material of the Fidel produce each time the astounding new combinations of sounds, words and statements, the atmosphere in the class becomes joyful, relaxed and is experienced as conducive of true learning. The class as a whole has been invited to cooperate; there are no weak and strong students, all help each other to improve their performance. In any case, because of the fact that no model has been offered, students know only what they are doing and see that some of the things they do make them capable of improving their performance. They cannot deny their own progress, collectively. They often enjoy the feeling that the group dynamics has brought them opportunities to be more effective faster.

Naturally the teacher who knows what he is pointing at can select his material for variety of intonation; for the production of many examples of the use of one word in different positions in a sentence; for a preparation of useful words to be met at the following stages and lessons, etc.

In particular, because there is no truth in languages but a criterion of "rightness," (i.e., the way natives sound things) the wise teacher may select statements to generate a feel for some of the habits in one language which may not belong to the vernacular of the class (if this exists) so that in the future only that which is in conformity with the selections, will sound right, not the students' own habits.

For instance the double negative "no nothing," is unacceptable in English, while the equivalent, "no hay nada," is required in Spanish. Hence a number of examples worked out via the pointer will establish what is right—either for English, if Spanish students are the class, or for Spanish, if English students form it.

Likewise the dropping or the repetition of conjunctions can be inserted in the examples worked out, and so on.

We shall see in the next two chapters how we can move beyond the stage of making utterances without reference to meaning, but here we want to stress the strange conclusion that meaning can be a hindrance, an interference, in the learning. When teachers test this approach in the classroom, they will know it at once. Theoretically it is obvious that, because students know nothing of the language and because the technique of pointing within the established conventions is capable of making students produce any number of statements in the new language, we have to make a decision about *a)* whether we shall practice what they have access to or *b)* postpone such exercises until the learned vocabulary is as extensive as what we ask of them.

Clearly this second choice is not ours: because it does not free the students, and because the activities we have separated need to be practiced in any case. Until now in other approaches they have been practiced together, but there are too few students learning languages in the world to prove the sound foundation of this approach. Our experiments have been spectacular and, even if only pragmatically, our choice is the one to be recommended because students gain a sense of what they have to do with themselves as utterers before embarking upon any other study requiring utterance *and* something else as well.

To sum up this chapter: the first one or two hours of teaching are devoted to the stringing of words on a Fidel. This will free students from their own habits of utterance and make them concentrate all their energies in making sense of how words and sentences should sound in the new language.

In the next chapter we shall introduce another booster closely linked to what we have considered so far but serving as a bridge to the introduction of meaning. Those who follow our advice will not have had to wait too long to reach what is their personal preferred choice of presentation.

3 The Next Step

If there is an order in the presentation of material to students, we shall find it by looking for exercises which will yield at the right moment a maximum for students' time.

Taking into account that, on the whole, the payment of each ogden yields only one remembered item, we can rarely obtain much advance in the learning of a language unless we link the ogdens paid to what one's intelligence can do with the retained items.

It happens that for most languages *numeration* has been structured so as to produce systematically the names of all numerals. Hence numeration will be a field of predilection for teachers who, like ourselves, are sensitive to the economics of learning and therefore of teaching.

Except for very young students, most students entering a second language will be familiar with numeration in their own language.

That is, the concepts will be readily available in their minds and will not require foreign language teachers to explain anything. Even when the figures for the numerals in their own language are not the Arabic ones, generally most students in our modern interdependent world will have had some exposure to the Arabic notation.

What we need to do here is to show how common sense dictates that numeration be the second set of exercises in a correct hierarchy of teaching a new language* in order for the best learning to be achieved as soon as possible.

Indeed, nowhere else is it possible to calculate as easily the cost in ogdens of a study whose importance cannot be denied and which, in addition, offers learners the first and most extended field of practice.

Let us study the question in the case of German although any language would do just as well.

Let us write in turn each figure from 1 through 9 on a horizontal line (spacing them so that there will be room between two successive figures for the insertion of up to two zeros without generating a continuous sequence).

    1   2   3   4   5   6   7   8   9

---

* In Hindi, common sense says to avoid teaching the numerals that early because of the high cost in ogdens.

3 The Next Step

Pointing to 1 after writing it, the teacher can either say *eins* or show the signs *ei, n, s* on the German Fidel. Students say it once or more times to ensure proper pronunciation. Then 2 is pointed to and *zwei* either said or shown on the Fidel. 3 and 4 can be treated in the same manner and then the four sounds (*eins, zwei, drei, vier*) thoroughly practiced. It is important to note that not all students seem to understand what they have to do with themselves to pay those four ogdens although they are evidently capable of it. Common sense tells us to avoid creating anxiety in those students and to ensure as much as possible that all of them master these four sounds, i.e., pay those four ogdens. Such remarks are dictated by experience. The rest is as easy, if not easier, since we are all retaining systems and natural payers of ogdens.

On a second line we shall either enter 10 (*zehn*) and have students say for no ogden payment *dreizehn* (13), *vierzehn* (14) *neunzehn* (19) leaving out for later 11 and 12 because they are irregular or giving them as *elf* and *zwölf for* two more odgens or enter 90 (*neunzig*) that cost one ogden for *zig* and let the students find 80 (*achtzig*) 60 (*sechszig*) 50 (*fünfzig*) 40 (*vierzig*) leaving out the irregular 20 (*zwanzig*) 30 (*dreissig*) and 70 (*siebzig*) or asking payment of three more ogdens. One more ogden is required for the word *und* to let the students say *drei und achtzig* for 83 and the pointed sequence: 3, und, 80. Examples of such numerals can be easily formed up to 99 (*neun und neunzig*) excluding perhaps 11 and 12

Hence for 17 (9 + 1 + 2 + 1 + 1 + 1 + 1 + 1) ogdens in all we can produce 99 German words or expressions.

Adding one more word *hundert* for one odgen we blow the boundary from 99 to 999; another, *tausend,* for one more ogden to 999,999. If *millionen* is practiced and these last two words: "Tausend millionen" (instead of *milliarden*), millionen millionen, etc., at no cost in ogdens. We can say: for only 20 ogdens students will get the means to utter any numeral, for example:

    123, 456, 789, 987, 654, 321, 666, 777, 888 as

    ein hundert drei und zwanzig millionen
       millionen millionen millionen

    vier hundert sechs und fünfzig tausend
       millionen millionen millionen

    sieben hundert neun und achtzig millionen
       millionen millionen

    neun hundert sieben und achtzig tausend
       millionen millionen

    sechs hundert vier und fünfzig millionen millionen

    drei hundert ein und zwanzig tausend millionen sechs hundert sechs und sechszig millionen sieben hundert sieben und siebzig tausend acht hundert acht und achtzig

or a sixty-five word utterance in the new language with full understanding.

3 The Next Step

Any student now has at his disposal a source of long statements in the new language, which can all be different and as challenging as one wishes, and upon which one will practice the sounds in the rhythmic manner asked for by that language. The longer the numeral, the better the preparation for a lengthy utterance that requires taking one's breath, molding the flow of sounds on specific demands due to the structure of the successive digits connected to their place and the triads, the successive triads punctuated by the mixtures of thousands and millions agreed to as the correct description of their place in the string of sounds. This complex discipline becomes second nature, and one can say after that short time that the novice students are as good as the natives in this matter. They have an experience in the new language in which they understand everything they say or hear said; where they know why they say what they say and do not need anyone's help to know whether they are right or where they have slipped and made a mistake.

Even if this were all one could gain from entering so early into such exercises, it would justify their adoption by all teachers. But there is much more in store.

Numerals are so prevalent in modern living that they form one set of words students will need constantly in many arrangements for: telling time, considering quantitative situations, giving one's address, one's telephone number, one's age, one's social security number, credit card numbers, license plate number, and so on, and they will serve students well in all these fields.

Arithmetic is one of the activities which people generally can do only in their native language, this need no longer be the case.

In fact mathematics is universal, and operations in arithmetic once understood, are valid in any language. If students can retain the names in the new language for the signs +, —, x, ÷, and =, they can give themselves that field as a whole as a practice area in the new language. Teachers can show on the Fidel the labels for those arithmetic signs and read universal statements such as: 7+9 = 16=9 + 7, or 16—9 = 7, or 16—7=9; and, putting zeros: 70+90= ; 160—70= , or 1600—700= , or 16,000—7,000=

Also: 2x3 = 6 and 6 ÷ 3=2; yielding 20x30=600, and 60,000 ÷ 300= ; and so on.

In all this, knowledge was brought by the students, and the items they must memorize cost them about 25 ogdens, while the yield is enormous and very important.

Soon, when some other basic items are learned, it will become easy to add in one hour or so of teaching, the socially important subjects of buying and paying in the new language, because this network of arithmetic is as available in the new language as in one's native tongue and sometimes better.

It seems to us that by so doing we are further freeing the students and showing common sense in our teaching.

4 Perception

We mentioned a number of times in the previous chapter that there was no truth in words and that the meanings associated with words come from another source. This source is the actual energy changes experienced by our system when it is submitted to either mechanical impacts (including those produced by voices that affect our eardrums), or electromagnetic impacts (including the photons that reach our retina), or heat and chemical impacts on our nerve endings.

All of these can add precise amounts of energy and represent the true contacts between our selves and the environment.

We are going to examine here how language is generated from perception and to use this finding to find out how we can take our students to the source of language so as to make them make sense of the choice of sounds that any group has produced over the years or centuries and has maintained that long for the purpose of saving energy.

The eyes of animals and men are affected by inputs of energy from the cosmos, inputs studied by physicists, who know more precisely than other people what color, hues and intensity are in terms of energy. Forms are associated with the areas of the retina which are affected by photons and generate awareness of shapes.

Forms, shapes and colors have a basis in fact, and we can speak of their truth, i.e., of what they generate in our sensitivity by their impacts; we can recall their truth by reactivating, actually or virtually, what the impact was.

Each of us in the environment can receive impacts upon the ears. These have also a truth in the complex energy distribution in which we can distinguish pitch, timber, intensity, stresses, and sounds because of our nervous equipment.

Our analytic equipment recognizes in a voice which maintains timbre, pitch, and intensity distinctions that come from the components of sounds, of which order is (a subtle) one. Our intelligence can recognize consistencies and stress them, thus giving them a reality amidst the whole package, also real in terms of energy. To perceive these subtle variations gives them a reality to which the self can become related.

The observations made by the self on two sets of perceptions are open to all those affected by energy changes and by the awareness that temporal changes also take place.

Hence each of us, drowned in reality and knowing truth directly can acknowledge that there is no truth in words but that there is truth in the consistency of the appearance of some words and some events affecting us. Because we learn as babies to talk to ourselves (in what has been refused the name of language), we know intimately that our vocal system can be linked to our hearing system and that we can transmute sounds made by ourselves into sounds heard and manage to peel off words from the voices we hear, including our own. The mental-physiological reality of words comes to us from the work we do in our crib, first with ourselves and later with the environment.

The two sets of perceptions that we embark upon in associating one with the other, can be associated because they are perceptions. Words can become a reality to which we can relate, but they are retained only when they trigger images, their meaning.

In fact, because we want to link a set of perceptions for which there is no other reality than our capacity to hold them as sounds in our memory and a reality to which truth is attached, we need to find ways of working that first bring the truth to the fore and then present an associated sign that can stand for that truth when consistently associated with it.

In our approach to language teaching it was found that a set of colored rods is a very good way of achieving that end. There are other objects no doubt that could be selected for the same end, but none seemed to be as versatile as these have been for the past many years. During that time, situation upon situation has been added to the point that I now know how to present, without any verbal explanation, most of the functional vocabularies of the languages I have come across.

To begin with, a generic term in every language is found to refer to each of the colored rods in a set, though it is not always easy to determine the most adequate vocable in the already existing vocabulary we examine.

Rod in English may be adequate for a 9 or 10 cm. prism, but only by an abuse of language does it apply to a cube 1 cm. long.

Khashaba first selected for Arabic but which describes more a plank than such a slender prism, has been coupled with twig, *oud*. But since words have only the meanings we give them, people have accepted our choices for the twenty languages we have worked on so far.

Hence we begin our presentation of the rods by picking a series of rods of different colors from the box, one at a time and in quick succession, without looking at anybody and saying as many times as we lift a rod the word selected for it. The student has therefore heard the same word associated with differing objects, what happens in their language obtains here again: i.e., that words apply to concepts, and concepts are classes. So "a rod," or its equivalent, is the label for any one of these objects in the same class.

Soon after, we lift one rod and name it by its color, clearly and loudly so that the position of the color attribute in the expression is evident, but no request is made for its repetition by the class. Instead a second rod is picked up, of different color and its name given. Only then are the students asked to name the first and, if successful (as they usually are) the second.

Students then know that they have been treated as retaining systems, that they can support each other in the task of paying ogdens for what is shown.

The teacher may be sitting at a table on which the set of rods is placed and on the other side of which is the class (made of any reasonable number of students that can be accommodated in the space available and can see the rods on the table). The rods are placed on the table, preferably standing, although no word is given for the position on the table at this stage.

The pointer is used to indicate which rod is to be named as the two names for the colors in the form relevant to the language studied (genitive adjective and nominative noun when needed, with an article used if the case applies) are practiced once or twice. A third, then a fourth, and up to nine different rods can be presented in turn, and each time one is introduced the pointer goes over the rods, the last one being pointed to alternately to give its name more occasions to be practiced. In some languages some labels are particularly demanding because a combination of sounds, or a length of words cannot be produced easily by the students. Rather than being avoided, they are introduced at an appropriate moment (not the first) and practice is given to them. This includes pointing on the Fidel, separating the syllables (we prefer to call them "beats") in the word so that each is indicated in order on a finger or on the rod itself and gone through, first slowly then more and more rapidly to encourage its correct production.

"Anaranjada" is such a word in Spanish, "momoilonobo" in Japanese is another, and "boortukaliya" in Arabic is a third example. We do not need to be troubled if such words are not produced perfectly in the beginning; there will be so many occasions to utter them and hence to work on them that they will become better pronounced by sheer attention to them and through constant use. Let us note that the teacher either points at the label for the color on the Fidel, saying nothing, or only gives the color in its right place in the sequence of words when students attempt to say its name.

When the nine rods introduced so far are standing together and the class in chorus produces the sounds for one of the permutations pointed to (there are almost a third of a million different choices for that operation of pointing), the teacher returns to the rods in the box and picks up two rods of the same color. Then he says loudly and clearly the words for two rods of such color or points on the Fidel to what the students need to say. Then instead of asking for this pair, he presents another pair and asks for the transfer of what has been learned so far to what has just been introduced.

Generally, languages display in their behavior awareness of change in the field of perception. Somehow the noises made convey that this statement, *two red rods,* differs from *a red rod.* This is the attribute of consistency mentioned earlier. Now, because of our study of numerals, we can use these as numeral adjectives and vary further the situations offered for students to verbalize. A sequence of noises connected to pointing to a set of rods standing on the table may elicit from the class "five yellow rods, two black rods, four red rods, a blue rod," etc.

Each language will suggest different forms as the common ones for the description of this set. *Rods* after the first in the series may be either dropped or replaced by a pronoun (*one* or *ones* in English). If *and* has been introduced as soon as two rods of two colors were held together and kept between the successive namings (as is demanded in Japanese) or only used once between the last two namings, we obtain one longish statement covering the description of a pointing at a set in which students have had to use themselves to do what natives of that language do, making changes for color, number, from noun to pronoun, or to silence, and using the conjunction in its proper place.

We must look at this situation more closely. We are at the beginning of our work, our students perceive the set in front of them and hold in their minds a small number of labels for which odgens have been paid (under the careful guidance of the teacher). Now they are made to use perceptions to trigger the appropriate sounds in the appropriate order and to do it knowingly observing the speed of speech, the correct pronunciation for each word, the right stresses, the running together of words that belong, and the pauses at the right places for the right durations producing an acceptable melody.

Until now it was words or signs in color that triggered the sounds of the new language. Now the triggering comes from objects and the variable attributes of number, of order (indicated by the movements of the pointer), of substitution of pronoun for noun, and of conjunction.

Students are operating in a complex manner in the new language, although we are just at the beginning. They do it well because it makes sense to them and, in fact, is easy.

They have been freed again in that no demand for memorization was made, but retention has been obtained because of their responsibility in the act of learning and the varied practice made possible when materials like the rods and the pointer are used. The Fidel remains handy so that previous learning is integrated with the new, each making its contribution in producing students as good as their teacher in the area covered.

In the same classroom the teacher will call two students to sit or stand on either side of him, preferable a male and a female student in order to convey the impact of gender upon words in the language being learned.

A preoccupation with feedback is another characteristic of the scientific approach we advocate in teaching. We want to keep our finger on the pulse and thereby make sure that what is heard from the students stems from them and is not merely a repetition of what the teacher says. Therefore, if verbs have to be brought in, action verbs and the imperative will serve best since

4 Perception

they show at once that there has been understanding by generating an unequivocal action.

The verbs we use in the beginning in all languages, are "pick up" or "take" "give" and "put." It is easy to make them plain without words of explanation. The first verb is made clear by saying to a student, *Take a — rod* or *take — — rods* and then taking his hand, putting it on top of the rod mentioned and closing his fingers on it. At once that student is induced by gestures to tell the other student, *Take —* (whatever he chooses).

The second student is induced to tell the first another of these forms in the singular and the teacher, holding his hand out, at once adds the equivalent of *Give it to me*. Then, turning to the other student, the teacher says, *Take . . . and give it to me*. If this order is executed he indicates by gesture to that student that he must give such an order verbally to the other student. If it takes place and the rod is received by the speaker, the teacher asks for that rod, and a round of *Give it to me* is formed. After going around one or two times the teacher introduces *Give it to him (or to her)*, or their equivalent forms in that language. The advantage of this new form is that the class as a whole can be involved and can tell any one of the three people at the table: *Take a — rod and give it to her (or him)* followed by a round of *Give it to her (or him)*. This can be coupled with the recipient's inserting *Give it to me* at the same time as the others make their statement.

We now have a number of options to consider. We can either go to the plural and replace *it* by *them,* if these exist in the language, or ask for a variety of rods to be picked up and given, some to one and some to another, as for example: *Take three blue rods and two black ones, give a black one to him and a blue one to me.*

This will lead to a situation that forces the introduction of the definite article (if it exists) and a new form such as "give me" instead of "give to me" (if it exists). The definite plural article (if it exists) can also be introduced by asking for more than one.

If the class has fewer than twenty students, we can involve each of them individually in telling neighbors to take rods and give themselves or others some of them. We only need to have a box of rods on hand and pass it from one student to the next until it returns to the table. To introduce variety the teacher can signal to the student ready to speak that he should ask for so many rods to be picked up and this many given to himself and that many to someone else nearby. In larger classes the students called to the table can be replaced at certain intervals by pairs or groups of other students, and the class can learn by proxy when the first personal pronoun is used but speak in chorus in the other cases.

With the verb *put* we can introduce *here, there* and the demonstrative adjectives and pronouns. For example: *Take seven rods, put one here, two there and give me three,* it is indicated by pointed where *here* and *there* should be.

After *this, that, these,* and *those* have been introduced with *put,* it is possible to introduce *is* and *are* (if they exist) and obtain sentences such as: *This rod is yellow and that one blue.* Or: *These rods are these two blue, this one white, and these three black.*

From there we can introduce: *The color of this rod is ...* or *The colors of these rods are ...* and start asking questions with *what*.

Possessive pronouns, adjectives, and the verb *to have* (if it exists) can be introduced as a cluster by having a few students and the teacher each holding, first, one rod (each a different color) with the teacher saying *My rod is blue* and each student in turn expressing possession in a similar manner. This is followed by the teacher's putting into circulation the equivalent of *his, her, their, our, your* and the corresponding forms for the pronouns.

By giving one or two students rods of the same color, we can introduce the equivalent of *too* or *also* with an immediate understanding of what is meant. *So is mine* can also introduce *so,* as an equivalent expression.

Then (or earlier) *another* and *the other* can be introduced, the first with *take,* the second with *give*.

Students can introduce themselves by saying *My name is ...* and soon after, their names can be used with personal pronouns, acting as objects in various combinations. Personal subject pronouns and the verb *to be* in the present, for *my name is ...* can be replaced by the equivalent expression: *I am so and so.*

This can be followed by *I am here, you are there* or *we are here and she is there*.

Now or earlier, occasions for the introduction of *not* or the negative form may have been met a number of times: *My rod is blue, it is not red* or *your rod is not yellow, it is orange*.

Yes and *no*, as part of an answer or in apposition, are easily put into circulation via: *Is his rod blue?* If the answer is affirmative *Yes* is sufficient while *no, it is yellow*, is the answer required in the negative.

If we think of teaching French, the pronoun *en* can be introduced quite early and be fully understood. In particular *je n' en ai pas,* claimed to be a major obstacle to non-French speakers, becomes obvious when practiced at this level.

Working with situations made with the rods brings to the classroom the naturalness found by babies in the home. The meanings come from the situations not from words and students seem ready to ask for the proper forms in the new language to fill in an expectation that somehow what one thinks should be sayable in this language.

The overall result is that there are no really difficult forms which cannot be illustrated through the proper situation involving rods and actions on them about which one makes statements by introducing specific words whose associated meaning is obvious. What teachers must do is to arrange for practice so that student's minds are triggered to use these new words spontaneously.

A rule we have followed in our work is to introduce, whenever possible, one new word or expression at a time and make it become second nature before the next one is introduced. This ensures that retention takes place without drill or idle repetition, that the ground is covered systematically, that more and more of the language is integrated, and that the students use the material freely and correctly, as natives do.

We shall see in the following chapters how the grammar of any language can be met empirically with sensitivity and confidence, not necessarily as verbal statements. These, however, can be easily formalized if required because one is aware of what one does with one's will and one's knowledge at this level of the behavior of the new language.

5 Independence, Autonomy and Responsibility

For a number of years our way of working, known as "The Silent Way," was notorious mainly because of the strange proposal that teachers should be silent when teaching language. Those who saw how effective a silent teacher could be, as compared to a teacher who talks a lot, gave silence a halo which needs to be removed.

Silence is not one teacher's bright idea: it has a definite place in teaching, neither more nor less than its reason for being there demands. Readers will understand this better if we go back to the suggestion made earlier that the aim of good teaching is to make students independent, autonomous and responsible.

Let us first make sure that we understand that we all have these attributes when we use our native language for everyday purposes to express ourselves and attempt to reach others through words.

Independence is the notion of our being aware that we can only count on ourselves. Since the instrument for our speech is made of somatic parts that are set into motion by our will, we already know, from the time we are very young babies, that only we ourselves can produce our sounds and that we can never ask anyone else to do it for us. As babies we therefore engage at once in the study of sound production and reach mastery of it in a few months. The awareness of our being in control is the source of our awareness of the ensuing independence.

Because we are born non-speaking, and because a quick examination places the language we shall learn in the environment, it is possible to make the mistake of thinking of each of us as totally dependent. In fact we are confusing two independent variables when we reach this condition of total dependence. The history of a group is generally unknown beyond a certain date, and no one can easily imagine how it came to speak that language and transformed it over historic time to what it is today. We are struck by one or two facts and leave the rest untouched. Deaf people have no access to the language of the environment. Hearing people hear themselves first and give themselves a frame of reference against which they make sense of sounds heard in order to command their speech organs to produce the equivalent of these. Each of us, again, stresses independence although we end up as a member of a group, as far as speaking is concerned.

5 Independence, Autonomy and Responsibility

Our independence results from our carrying within ourselves all that is required to learn any existing language. Ancient and dead languages are picked up from manuscripts stored in shelves in libraries, which are not an environment for everyone but only for those who know how to dig into them.

We can therefore grant our students that they know how to be independent learners even before we meet them in our classroom. If they are hearing people, this recognition will allow us to use their ability with the spoken language in our work with them. Those of us who do so partake in the spirit of The Silent Way.

As soon as we find that we are all capable of using not only what we hear people say around us but also the transforms which occur to us in the various circumstances of our life, we demonstrate our autonomy in addition to our independence. Each of us knows that the kind of retention asked for by the native language is the one capable of being triggered, i.e., that of recognition rather than that of faithful memory, with total conformity.

It is a fact open to every observer, including young children, that since every one can become a user of the language spoken in the environment, that language must be, by construction, accommodating to all people living in and experiencing so many varied circumstances.

Words refer to classes, not to individuals. Classes are by definition vague in order to allow the inclusion of individuals, which can have, besides the property that makes them members of that class, any number of properties which separate them from each other. Buttons, for example, are referred to as buttons for one property, and this does not exclude their being shiny or dull, round or square or oblong, metal or plastic, being of any particular color, embossed or flat, and so on.

Everybody can use the word "I," say, which is so singular by convention, although it does not evoke a class.

Words are known not only as sounds, as stressed syllables linked to unstressed ones, as being capable of linking with other words, as having some functions in the various sentences into which they can be incorporated, but also as triggers of meanings. Ambiguity seems to be inevitable in this last operation because the triggering is not of one and the same thing, neither for everyone nor for all the time. The use of words for expression does not necessarily imply their use for communication. It is possible to use words deliberately to mislead, and this compatibility between speech and lying can serve as a basis for the distinction between expression and communication, as it is between truth and consistency. The first—expression—is a power of the mind, the second—communication—an event with a certain probability attached to it, a probability that can be zero, as in disguising one's thought, and is almost never 100%.

Because of this span, we can recognize that, while expression is capable of improvement through a better acquaintance with what a language can do, communication can only improve when a set of circumstances come together; first, when the originators of the statements pay attention to expression and see to it that what is said is not misleading; second, when the recipients of the statements do receive them for what they are, i.e., when they have learned to listen in order to receive rather than to interfere; third, when the recipients can make sense of what they have heard; and, fourth, when they can make the same sense as, or come sufficiently close, to that of the speaker.

This set of circumstances is almost impossible at will, although it may happen and, perhaps, often happens. Because of this we can safely say that in verbal relationships "communication is almost a miracle."

The autonomy of speakers is the outcome of the existence of choices of expressions available to them. Every language offers equivalent expressions, and their mere existence says that speakers are given the freedom to make choices within the language. These choices can be found in the expressions since these are triggered by realities. For instance, we can all say either: "I am on your right." or "You are on my left." The choice exists because there are two starting points. Once made, the choice imposes the words, and in these words we can find what caused the choice.

Equivalent expressions also exist to tell us that language is not memorized, that if a word is not triggered one's mind can substitute others in its place, perhaps several at once, in a sentence or a statement. The facility of producing equivalent expressions restates again and again our autonomy in our use of our language.

If these are properties of how we assimilated our native language, they cannot be neglected in our teaching of a second language without a loss for our students.

And there is a third component in our use of language, the one we call responsibility. Clearly we are first responsible because we have a will and it is being used when we say something or refrain from saying anything.

We are also responsible in what we do in preparing for the utterances. Although we have at our disposal automatic mechanisms that smooth the triggering of words, we cannot say that they just jump out of our mouth. Above and beyond these mechanisms there are the workings of the mind, which select from among all that can rush to consciousness the items for which we know there are expressions and let these items trigger the words. We are selective and therefore responsible for the selection.

This raises in each of us the criterion of the adequacy of the selection to the intention. Babies know their responsibility, and this helps them in their selective retention of vocabulary. In any given situation they can perceive that they have not established an association and do not have a particular label for it. They then watch others in similar situations, extract from the speech heard one or more words, and at once give themselves a chance to use it. The outcome of this test will decide on whether to hold on to the finding or pursue the research. The so-called "abstract words" (as if any were not abstract!) obviously require this working.

5 Independence, Autonomy and Responsibility

For instance, the expression "I might" can be felt to be adequate when one senses that a particular situation offers a margin of choice and that one feels inclined to make it.

Each of us develops inner criteria in order to cope, in the virtual, with all the substitutes for experience. Language is part of this arsenal. Its functionings include besides the actual mobilization of part of the self to own its vocabulary, its structures, its expressions (colloquialisms), the many triggerings at different depths and the connections to one's will. Inner criteria are criteria of the self even though, in so many of us, they work smoothly and seem automatic, thus hiding the presence of consciousness.

Because, as teachers, we are aware of all the above, we can make proposals that do subordinate teaching to learning.

Our techniques and materials are profoundly related to these awarenesses, and we deplore the fact that students of The Silent Way see either only silence or only rods as the contribution to language teaching of this prolonged research.

If we go back to the previous chapters, it will be seen that we let each student be responsible for his or her choice of the sounds to produce, either when the pointer runs over signs of the Fidel or when perceptible attributes of a situation with the rods trigger them.

This use of responsibility leads to independence, but it would not be sufficient to guarantee it. The coloring of the signs on the

Fidel (and on the wall charts as we shall soon see) gives the students means to exercise their independence since the contact with truth, recognized through perception, is the basis for all retention. Moreover, the existing channels in the mind and the brain are made deliberately available to give the self the feelings that one's resources are at one's disposal and not only memorized elements that operate with uncertainty because they exist thanks to others.

We have cultivated autonomy in so far as choices were deliberately put into situations and students allowed to make them and particularly in generating a climate of flexibility in the new language which—like the vernacular—is also ruled by equivalent expressions.

Every language has its own idiosyncrasies and each one must be treated singularly. Still, all are handled apparently in the same way: for all of them we use colored Fidels, word charts with words in color, colored rods, and pointers. The appearance can be carried even further since the teacher is silent on so many occasions, the classes are managed in the same ways, the content of so many charts are simple transpositions from one language to another, and since the same pictures are part of the various kits, the same worksheets go with them. Even the three books included in the materials can be considered as part of the uniform way of treating all languages although a quick examination of one of them: "A Thousand Sentences," will reveal that, as the various languages are connected to different cultures, these introductions of the everyday vocabulary used in each culture are very different.

The truth there, as usual, goes beyond the appearance. All of our materials are instruments; it is their uses that form the lessons we give. We saw that each Fidel is the summary of all the sounds and all the spellings of each language, which of course, differ from one another as much as men have decided to make them in the various areas of the world. But all of them present the students with the panorama of the components of the language being studied. The Fidels are more informative than Mendeleïev's Table is for chemists, for we cannot produce chemical compounds by linking the names of the atoms to one another with a pointer while we can induce the sounds of the native language that way.

By coloring with the same hues as many of the signs carrying the same sounds on the various Fidels, we have on the one hand, stressed the value we attach to independence by opening the new language through what one knows of one's own and, on the other hand, generated a climate of optimism in seeing that all languages are linked at that fundamental level of the component sounds.

By the consistency of coloring on the word charts, we have made our students independent. They can decode by themselves in any script several hundred selected words because these are sufficient to convey through special combinations all the structures of the language in question, as well as to provide practice of the essential vocabulary of that language (cf. next chapters).

But our selection of what to put in the various charts is intimately related to the demands of each particular language, which may be very different from those of languages the students already know.

Above all we want students to behave spontaneously like native speakers. We can only achieve this by generating in them all the inner criteria which are automatically at work in the natives. These criteria will make them responsible and autonomous. Hence we begin with what is unique in the new language that makes it so different.

Our use of the rods to create situations frees the students from having to guess what words mean and from translating, since the truth that triggers the words has been made visible and students can concentrate on the verbal material put into circulation and on becoming swift, accurate, and intelligible to others through clear and correct sounds.

One of the remarkable findings that comes from working in this way is the ease with which the students' minds relate only to the new language, by locking the mechanism that triggers all the others. So, the native languages of the students can be as varied as possible, without affecting what goes on in the learning. All students, whatever their origin, are treated alike.

Students know that they do not make up the language they are studying. They know that they have no right to ask it to behave differently from the way it is shown to them. They accept that "rightness" rather than truth justifies its usage and move as quickly as possible towards accepting the idiosyncrasies of the new language.*

This surrender to the reality of the contrived system that any language is makes for much easier assimilation of the so-called difficult peculiarities of languages. Hence from the start, i.e., from the content of chart 1, we offer practice with the presence or absence of gender, of declensions, of verbal accords, of plurals, of pronouns, of many adjectives, of prepositions and conjunctions, of the very functional vocabulary which permits every one of the structures of the language, however complex, to be formed. Though restricting the vocabulary, we found that we do not have to restrict the language met by the students.

This discovery that the vocabulary we have to teach (i.e., involve students in) can be made of only a few hundred words has led to the postponement of the expansion of vocabulary and the insistence that our responsibility as teachers is to make students function and not to store statements that might be useful, for example, in some special aspect of a trip. Making students function is linked with making them free. Once functioning, they will retain much more easily sets of words which are relevant in certain ways, as they prove when we present them with the pictures or the book of "A Thousand Sentences."

To ease the study of the functional vocabulary with the rods and charts will be the object of the next chapter. To close this chapter

---

* This wisdom has been mistaken for imitation, particularly in the case of babies, although no one can actually learn to speak by imitation.

let us repeat that we only use silence when it is appropriate; if such is often the case, it is only because it is the students who have to do the work to own a language and we should let them do it without interference.

But we use so much more than silence in The Silent Way! It is the way of sensitive, responsible teachers who know that their job is to be on the side of learners. All the time. So that these learners relate to the language, to its demands, and to the rewards which came from finding their endowments capable of being used in another fashion which reveals to them the competent learner each of them is, or at least has been.

Learning a language thus goes beyond acquiring new behaviors: it is one more step towards being a freer person.

6 Uses of Rods and Charts

While the same box of rods can serve for the teaching of any language, each language requires its own set of charts. Since it is not very useful to fill pages with reproductions of these in a book such as this which is devoted to the teaching of all languages, we shall consider here only what can be done with the rods and state that words corresponding to activities with the rods go into the successive charts.

Because students must have a certain number of words and they need to learn them to make sentences, choices of which words to place together on the charts necessarily arise. There are words that are very special, such as the name of a specific tool used by, say, a dentist. To give it space on the word chart would mean that that space is no longer available and that the word will be used only when sentences involving the name of that object are selected. In contrast, a personal pronoun seems to be asked for in many sentences on a vast number of occasions.

Space on wall charts is at a premium, and, since the charts are meant to be displayed in classrooms and to be seen from up to ten meters away, they cannot accommodate more than 40 words a piece. Twenty charts occupy as much wall space as is usually available in a classroom. Hence 800 words are as many as we can hope to have on such colored word charts, and, in fact, what we offer is about 500 words in 12 charts, leaving room for the Fidel charts (8 of which are needed in the case of English and French, one to four in the case of other languages).

The space on a chart of 16x22 square inches (40x55 sq. cm.) can be used in a number of ways for up to 40 words. On the whole, we avoid repetition with the exception of the chart devoted to numeration, which can be used alone and, therefore, may have to contain words from other charts. But it is also possible to be economical by placing, near the edges of the charts, endings which can be used with many stems to produce various verb tenses and paradigms, adverbs, declensions, and so on.

Of course, since pronouns are more economical than nouns, all pronouns are given, but very few nouns are included (unless in a particular language they can also be used for other functions, as is the case for English and Arabic).

We described in Chapter 4 how we introduce the rods and why we use the imperatives of action verbs. We can now observe that since it is possible to get the students to retain these words and to say spontaneously to one another: "take — and give — ," using singular and plural pronouns, and since they can increase (a) the number of the sentences merely by using substitutions, (b) their length by using the conjunction, and (c) their variety by using negation and some of these combined, the roles of chart 1 are several:

- to relieve memory by keeping the words in the view of the students,

- to support memory by making available the needed words and through the color code, their sounds,

- to indicate that substitutions are possible, by providing first one structure for a sentence and then several additional sentences with this structure,

- to provide a number of structures which are immediately usable and understandable, though invisible on the charts,

- to offer the possibility of dictating visually sentences to be read, acted upon, or written by the students,

- to offer the possibility for testing that students can make sentences, correct ones in the new language, and can order other students to do things that are of a certain level of complexity (such as taking certain rods and giving them to a certain number of people in a certain way and a certain order),

- to offer the possibility of seeing that the language associated with a definite set of words depends on the imagination of the user and not on the number of words used.

What is learned with chart 1 will serve again when more charts are added. All that follows is expansion. Students can say more and more and express many more relationships in the new language. These relationships are concerned with people involved in space and time, in cause and effect. The people have names, sizes and positions in space and time relative to other people or places, in a culture that quantifies and qualifies. Hence the charts offer clusters of words which permit one to refer to the present, the past, and the future, to conditions, doubts, guesses; to space, orientation, location, distance, shape and position; to temporal relations, simultaneity, order, duration; to tell the time, the date, to quantify; to count, to distribute and share; to relate to words, telling, saying, showing, explaining, asking, answering; to modulate expressions via adverbs, to describe, to narrate, to question, to discuss, etc.

When we say that the rods serve to bring students an awareness of how one says something in a particular language what one already knows how to perceive and how to express in another language, we have in mind uses of oneself with the rods in one's hand in order to create a situation (static or dynamic) which conveys the idea while the words are spoken or pointed out on the charts.

It is easy to see how the words "at the same time" and "simultaneously" can be made plain simply by using two hands to pick up two rods or two sets of rods, contrasting the situation and, therefore, the words that show "one after the other" or "successively."

It is easy to see that if one talks before acting one refers to intention, hence to the future, while talking when acting requires the present, and talking after the action, the past. So it is possible to cluster the three tenses in one situation, distinguishing clearly between them and thus eliminating confusion between conjugations. Practice will be given as follows.

The convention for "thinking about" by holding either one hand on one's brow or a finger at one's temple, will be introduced as a gesture preceding an action. The words uttered for this preparation or shown on the Fidel or the charts correspond to the English "I am going to . . . " The action verb is added as: "take one by one (or two by two) the — rods" or "make a wall or a road or a plan for a house" etc., or "heap the yellow rods" or "throw . . . rods" and so forth.

When entering the action there will be no need for a convention, the perception will make clear what "now, I am taking or making or throwing . . . " means. Once done, again with the conventional gesture of a job having been finished, the words uttered would be "I took or made or threw or heaped . . . "

The teacher may need to do up to four of these sequences to establish the basic forms. Then a student is asked to take the teacher's place and to go through the sequence above in a silent mimicking of what was done before, in order to prove that he can recall and act out the expressions of intention, of being involved in the action, and of finishing that action.

The teacher asks the student to repeat this scene and says: "He or she is going to take . . . " followed by "he or she is taking . . . " followed by "he or she took . . . " Joining the student he will introduce "we are going to . . . " etc. Putting two students at the table will yield "they are . . . " etc.

When one or two students form the object of description, "he or she" or "they" become "you" as soon as the teacher, instead of pointing at him or them while facing the class, turns to the students and addresses them directly.

Clearly this would not have been necessary if on an earlier occasion the subject pronouns had been introduced. The class could prove that it knew how to work out the appropriate element in the paradigm, by making all the transfers of words according to the situation.

This kind of practice offers multiple advantages for the learners. First it makes them meet the pronouns together, know when to use which one, rather than having to remember an order in a conjugation. Second, because they have had to adapt each one to a situation with visible indicators that trigger some words and not others, they are articulating a set of utterances rather than unrolling a memorized paradigm. Third, they distinguish the parts of the statements that refer to time and go to form the structure of the sentences from those that are variable because of the action. Fourth, it makes them able to tabulate, if need be, their observations of how the language links the intention with the infinitive of the variable verb, the processing of the action with the gerund, and the accomplished action with the past participle (in the Romance Languages, or the Germanic, at least), thus generating a feel for these grammatical entities to be used for future reference when studying the behavior of the language.

The rods are a vehicle for any language. The teacher who knows a given language will want to put in the set of charts the items that can go with the illustrations offered by the situations constructed with rods and which provide the students with the encounter of the specific demands of that language. Hence the charts become another instrument that we can use to free the students. They cannot do much by themselves since they only show colored words, but the using of the pointer will force students to say what the natives say, without translation though not, however, without an illustration to generate understanding if this is possible either by using rods or the members of the class.

The job of selecting the words and the endings that allow one to adapt to gender, case, number, tense, mood, etc., is the most important one, and a science exists for just this purpose. It says that, if we want people to function in the new language, we must first give them the *functional vocabulary, i.e., the items which generate the grammar of the language.* These items are the ones we find in any article or passage when we cross out most of the nouns, many of the adjectives and a number of the verbs; what is left refers to one's self and to others in the numerous relationships of everyday life. We can therefore decide fairly easily what to put on our list.

In all languages chart 1 contains, as described in Chapter 4, the names for the colors of the rods (including or not words for light or dark), the word for rod, the means to make the plural, the verbs to take, to give, to put, in the imperative; personal pronouns; possessive, demonstrative adjectives and pronouns, in some languages question words.

Charts 2 and 3 add to these words the rest of the pronouns (relative, interrogative, personal, indefinite), and the words for *here, there, of, for*. The word for *name* is used to make the personal involvement of students in their statements possible as well as to allow members of the class to make the acquaintance of others they do not know. If desired, forms of introduction can be linked with this. In some languages these words also introduce reflexive verbs.

Chart N, (sometimes called Chart 4) is devoted to the numerals. We considered its use in Chapter 3. This chart could also be called number 0 since it does so often come before Chart 1 in providing students with fluency *and* total comprehension of a chunk of the language.

Chart 5 can be devoted to space relations and the numerous words describing them. The rods are ideal for this introduction since it is so easy to place two rods *side by side, on top of each other, behind* or *in front of each other, face to face, back to back, on the side, on the left of* or *the right of, between others, closer,* or *farther*.

6 Uses of Rods and Charts

Comparing sizes gives opportunities for comparatives and superlatives.

Chart 6 can be devoted to temporal relations rendered in English by: *now, later, after, before, at the same time, while, soon, till, yet, when,* and *through*. Interspaced with these words in Charts 4, 5, 6 are words referring to order, causality, dependence, condition, age, similarity, differences, quantifiers (*a few, several, some, many, all*), signs that can produce adverbs from adjectives, gerunds from verb roots. So whenever possible, rods are used, but they are not always adequate; for example, to indicate what *young* or *old* are. We can cither postpone introducing these words until pictures are introduced or, when possible, use people in the class or who can be brought to the class.

The purpose of Chart 7 is to bring shades of meaning that adverbs reflect, and, since adjectives with a certain ending often become adverbs, this chart also procures the opportunity of increasing the number of qualifiers. Charts 8 and 9 are devoted to completing the presentation of verbs with special reference to complicated cultural variations if these exist (as in Hindi, Korean, Japanese, Thai, for example).

Chart 10 is given to family relationships, Chart 11 to time and the calendar, Chart 12 to seasons and other references to days, weeks, months, years.

In some languages a large, important vocabulary refers to the quantifiers that go with numerals and are specific words without which one will create confusion. These quantifiers occupy a special chart in Japanese, Korean, Chinese, and Thai, and often follow the chart for numerals. For this chart rods are not adequate since only one quantifier would apply to them. Actual objects to which they refer are needed and must be brought to the classroom.

In spite of these special restrictions, rods are still the most valuable instrument we have ever found because their quantity, mobility, size, variety and uniformity make them implicitly capable of generating equivalent expressions. And this creates autonomy in the students. Rods form classes. Some are classes of equivalence (all the yellows, all the reds . . .), some are orders (from the tallest to the shortest, from the smallest to the largest . . .), some are multiples or fractions (doubles and halves, triples and thirds . . .), some are geometrical classes (squares, rectangles, prisms, cubes, trains, walls, perimeters, areas . . .).

The rods can be used to measure, to produce diagrams (clocks, outlines of rooms, furniture, houses, parks, benches . . .), even to represent people, as for example, one can be called Ms. or Mr. Black and another Mr. or Ms. Green or Mr. Brown and moved around on a table as marionettes among other rods representing trees, arches, gates, etc.

In the next chapter we shall see how we can exploit the words on the charts. Here we want to illustrate how the rods serve the three purposes of introducing the perceptible trigger for a few functional words, of making subtle distinctions visible, of extending the rods to life situations.

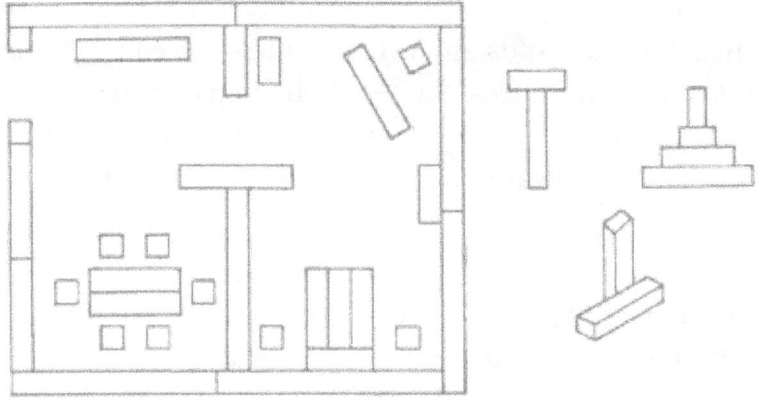

A. Examples of Introducing Triggers for:

1 A Cluster of Expressions in Space Relations

The teacher while sitting at his desk in front of the class, holds two rods vertically, a certain distance apart. By moving his hands, he can move them either closer together or further apart. This command upon the distance can be associated with the following statements: "These two rods are a certain distance apart—now they are closer—now they are much closer—they are very close—they are very, very close—they are side by side almost against each other—now, they are against each other—now they are taken apart—further apart— still further and further—now they are far apart—now, they are very far from each other—now they are as far as they can be (when held in this way)—now they are moving towards each other—they are less far than before—they are coming fast closer to each other, still at a certain distance—now, they are not too far from each other—the distance between them is diminishing— they are going to bang on each other—they collide." Repeating these accordion-like movements of the hands and arms, the teacher can get from the class the above utterances. Students can help each other to recall all these expressions and practice them until all can feel confident to describe any such situation.

When two smaller rods are used on the table to represent two cars on a highway, the same vocabulary applies to the description of their mutual spatial connections, the only addition being the word "car."

2 A Cluster of Expressions in Temporal Relations

The teacher, while sitting at his desk with the set of rods in front of him, picks up rods: very slowly—less slowly—faster—still faster—very fast —madly fast. Then he picks up some rods and drops them: continuously—sporadically—from time to time—one at a time—a few at a time with each hand—alternately—simultaneously—rhythmically. Alternatively he can pick up: first a blue—then a yellow—then three red—now an orange—later a black—still later two more black ones—finally a white one.

After the event the following statement can be made "to begin with he took two brown ones, later three white ones, one at a time, then a few rods all together and dropped them sporadically two by two. Finally he took a handful of rods and put them back in the box."

3 Some Causes and Effects

"If I place this rod vertically on top of this rod standing on the table, will it stay?—let us try—it does." "Now what if I place another rod?—let us try—I must be careful.—it does." "Now if I placed a third rod, will it stay?—it might." "If I am lucky and very careful, it might.—It does." "Do you think that if I . . . —No, no chance!—it fell as you predicted." "Did it fall because I was not careful, I was clumsy or because the ends are not perfectly cut?"

Repeating the same situation could give opportunities for students to describe it using *him* and *he* or *her* and *she* or *the teacher* and also *them* for the rods. The teacher can force the recall of *be careful; don't be clumsy; if he is lucky,* or some statement like: "Let us predict how many can stand vertically one upon the other," by using white, red, green or pink rods, which are easier to stack.

B. Making Subtle Distinctions Visible:

1 While, At the Same Time, Simultaneously, During
Again the situation is the same as in A (2) or (3)

"I'll take rods with my two hands—while I take blue rods with my right hand, with my left I'll take red ones—while I take some rods, I shall stand up (sit down)—while I take some rods, I shall speak—can I point at words while I pick up rods with my two hands?—and with one hand?" will elicit: "If you are careful you can pick up rods with one hand while you point at words on the chart with the other;" "I'll take rods one by one at the same time with each of my two hands and choose them: (a) to be of the same color—or (b) to be each time of a different color—or (c) to be of the same color for my left hand and of a different color each time for my right hand" and elicit the appropriate expressions from the class with "you" replacing "I." The teacher orders: "Take simultaneously one rod with each hand, do it several times over and each time put your rods simultaneously on either side of the heap (or box)."

"While Mary picks up rods for John, he will go round the table and during that time we shall all look only at Mary. While John was going round the table we were looking at Mary, who during that time was picking up rods for John. At the same time as Mary picked up rods, we looked at her and John went round the table; during that time the clock showed a one minute shift of the hands which simultaneously registers the movement of the sun in the sky. The sun seems to go round the earth, while it is the earth that goes round the sun."

2 Because, For, As, Though, Since, Before, Already, Then

Again as in A (2) or (3) and B (1)

"Give me one.—Now I have three since I had two before.—Because you gave me one and I already had two, I now have three.—I had two, you gave me one, I now have three, for two and one make three.—Though before I had only two, I now have three because you gave me one.—Since I had two before and you gave me one, I now have three.—I already had two, then you gave me one and now I have three."

"Why do you want so many red rods?—Because this rod is a blue one, it takes four red rods and one white one to make a train as long as the blue."

"Since the blue rod is as long as a brown rod plus a white one, and since a brown rod equals a train of four red rods, we want four red rods and one white one to make a train as long as a blue rod."

"Because a blue rod equals nine white ones end to end and two white rods make a red one, we want four red and one white rod for a blue one."

"As a blue rod is bigger than a brown one by one white rod, we will need a white rod at the end of a red train to make it as long as a blue rod since a brown rod is equal to a train of four red rods." "Though we can make longer and longer trains with red rods, we need a white rod at the end of a red train to make it as long as a blue rod."

"Because the blue rod is longer than the brown, and because a white rod is half as long as a red one, we need four and a half red rods to make a length equal to that of a blue rod."

"Since two whites equal one red, one white equals half of a red."

"As we cannot make red trains equal to a blue rod we need a white rod after four red ones to make a train equal to a blue rod."

3 If, Whether, Supposing

"If you take a handful of rods out of this box whether one of them is a white one depends on whether you scrape the bottom or not.—If I saw well, you took a red rod.—Whether I know that you have taken a red rod depends on if I was looking when you did it."

"Supposing your hand was twice as long could you hold in it twice as many rods?"

"If I were twice as big would my hands also be twice as long?—Whether hands become bigger in the same proportion as the body, I do not know.—Whether by supposing this, we reach the truth is a big if.—With if's anything becomes possible."

"Whether man is an animal is a difficult question."

"Tell me whether or not you are coming, for if you come I need to buy more food, this supposing you come early enough to eat with me."

C. Extending to Life Experiences

1 A Clock

Measuring the yellow rods with white ones the students will be able to tell that there are five whites in a yellow. Multiples of 5 are then named, i.e., 10, 15, 20, 25, 30, 35, 40, 45, 50, 55, 60, when a train made of yellow rods is formed to stop at twelve rods. A quick manipulation by the teacher will turn this train into a "regular" dodecagon and students can read the rods as 1, 2, 3 ... up to 11 and 12.

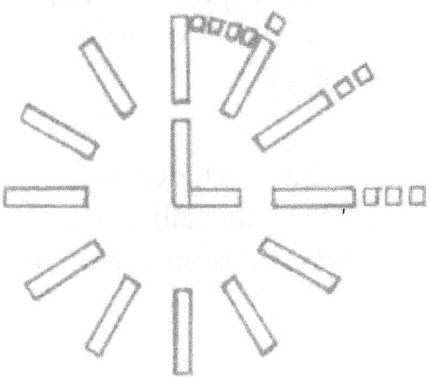

Placing a blue rod so that it joins the center of the dodecagon and the vertex marked twelve, we can expect that students will figure out that it is the minute hand of a clock. A black rod placed at the center may represent the hour hand.

The following statements can now be made: "This is a clock.—We can see on it what time it is.—This is the hour hand, this is the minute hand.—If I place the blue rod like this and the black one like that, we say it is three o'clock.—Now, what does the clock show?—Seven o'clock." (or any of twelve different possibilities.)

A student can be called and told: "Place the hour hand so that the clock shows two o'clock" (or eleven other possibilities which can be given to students to show). In case of error, reference to other students is helpful, the teacher coming in as a last resort.

Then with the black rod left in a fixed position pointing towards any vertex, the blue rod can be shifted from vertex to vertex until it is returned to the "o'clock" position. When this happens the black is made to jump to the next vertex (clockwise), and the movement of the blue repeated.

The language of time thus includes various modes of telling time, before and after the hour, half, quarter, three quarters, of an hour, a third of an hour (in some languages), a.m., p.m., 1-24 hour time.

It can now be said that the students are using numeration and their functional vocabulary to master the local usage of telling time and are therefore as good as their teacher in that area.

2 The Calendar

Since black rods are seven times as long as white ones, we can represent each week by a black rod and each day by a white one, making the first day of that week a Sunday (airlines use Monday as first day) or the conventional religious day following the Sabbath.

With Sunday (or Monday) as the start of the first month, every month of the solar year (or the lunar or the lunar-solar year) can be represented by four black rods placed side by side along with another rod whose length completes the number of days (30 or 31) of the month announced.

Months can be labeled from January to December (or any other names used in a language or culture), terms and seasons defined and labeled with their corresponding months and dates of start and finish. Fiscal years, religious and national festivals can be treated similarly.

Students can be made to write their date of birth and read to themselves or aloud to others in the new language. Additional words such as "I was born on the . . . " "I will celebrate my next birthday on . . . " "I must remember that my mother was born on . . . , my father or my sister on . . . , my brother(s) on . . . " (my in-laws could perhaps be added).

3 Today, Yesterday, Tomorrow, etc.

This lesson could be given before or after the one on the calendar. The results may be different for one or the other because both use the days of the week but not in the same way.

Rods are selected and can serve best if the lesson is given by the teacher from the table in front of a large class.

During the clock lesson the equivalence "one day is another name for twenty-four hours" could have easily been understood. Similarly, "in a duration of twenty-four hours we count a night and a day.—The middle of a day is called *midday,* the middle of the night *midnight.*"

"*Noon* is a name equivalent to 12 o'clock, but can also refer to a duration around that hour.—*Midnight* is a name for 24 o'clock, or 0 o'clock."

In some cultures before noon, or a.m. (in Latin), and afternoon, or p.m. refer to different usages: before noon is called *morning* if the sun is up and *a. m.* covers the part of the night before sunrise and after midnight. *Afternoon* can be used for a few hours after noon, but never after sundown, which is the *evening*. Evenings become *night* around the conventional bedtime of around 10 p.m. in summer.

If it is still before midnight, the day after midnight is called *tomorrow*. After midnight, the day before midnight is called *yesterday*.

Having introduced *yesterday* and *tomorrow* and the clock, the teacher can place an orange rod standing on the table and say "today is . . . ;" then places another orange rod on its left, he says "yesterday was . . . " and yet another one on its right, "tomorrow is . . . " This situation can be practiced before another rod is placed at the right of the one for tomorrow to represent "the day after tomorrow" and one placed to the left to the one for yesterday for, "the day before yesterday." To complete a week the teacher places two more rods, one on the right (and called "the day following the day after tomorrow"), and one on the left (called "the day preceding the day before yesterday").

These orange rods can be placed side by side on top of a black rod which then represents a week. The names of the days of the week could be re-introduced now in conjunction with their mutual relations.

Exercises such as: "if yesterday was . . . , what will tomorrow be?" and variations on this will link the two clusters and provide practice.

4 Various Plans of Houses, Schools, Hospitals, etc.
Such plans can be made with rods and filled with objects represented by rods. These situations can be treated like any other made with rods and of which students have had plenty of experience. A need for words, other than the functional vocabulary practiced so far, will arise and the teacher may put them into circulation: "Let us make a *plan* of a *garage*" say. The situation can be described while being made by: "Here are the three *walls* and here the *entrance,* a *door* that can be *lifted,*" as long as it is clear that the symbolic use of the rods is grasped by the students.

Then any number of developments are possible. One of them could be "The people who live here do not have a *car*. They use the garage space to *store goods,*" and a number of rods would be placed inside the rectangle made of rods. They put a *wardrobe* here to store their *clothes* when they are out of season; here they have a *bench* for *woodwork* with *tools* hanging on the wall." The teacher can of course touch his or her clothes when the word appears, act as if planning or sawing a plank when woodwork and tools appear, or stretch on the table to evoke the meaning of bench and so on.

If a car is used instead, one of the smaller rods can be used for a *compact car,* a longer one for a *custom station wagon.* Speaking of comings and goings, of shopping, taking children to school, or traveling by road will produce opportunities for use of the functional vocabulary and the successive insertion of new words connected with everyday life.

Clearly a plan of a house will be a situation readily accessible, with bedrooms, patio or garden, lawn (or absence of these for city apartments) and the furniture and equipment vocabulary available.

Producing a plan of the classroom in which the lesson is taking place can involve the class and will include a lot of vocabulary to describe what goes on in it. The students and the teacher enter. They go to their *seats,* the first may be behind *desks* or sitting in *chairs* with *writing facilities.* A *chalkboard* (since *eraser* and *chalk* are in the classroom, they can be labeled and shown) can be made by piling up a few black rods on top of a yellow support. A teacher standing in front of it calls students' attention to what he or she is putting on it, and so on.

Because of the ease with which the rods can enter into model making, there is no end to their use in the extension of the symbolic situations of everyday life. Teachers can become experts in such inventions and produce the vocabulary required beyond the functional one that is associated with the charts. Pointing at signs on Fidels will even leave to the students the responsibility of putting the needed words into circulation. But they can often as validly be uttered by the teacher and immediately used by the students.

Associated with such uses of the rods are the uses of the pictures and worksheets and of the book "A Thousand Sentences" described in detail in Chapter 9. Teachers are free to use or not to use the existing connections between these materials and the rods. According to the level of the classes and the reason for studying the new language, it will be thought advisable to make the association just mentioned, or not.

The next chapter will be a return to the charts *per se* and will place a distance between the topics just studied and their treatment outside the charts. Perhaps readers will care to look at the relevant chapters before entering the next one.

7 Exploiting the Functional Vocabulary

We have seen why the particular words that go on the charts were chosen. We have seen how they are kept available to the students so they don't have to fear forgetting any of them, and also how those words can be associated to meanings illustrated by situations with the rods and met in one or more uses practiced in the classroom. Hence the words on the charts trigger at least one meaning and, when incorporated in sentences, may trigger more than one.

For instance, words introduced as nouns may sometimes be used as verbs (ex., *name*); adjectives can produce adverbs (ex., *short* becomes *shortly*) or even serve as nouns (ex., *black*) or verbs (*brown*); and verbs become nouns (ex., *take*),

This kind of situation can be made into a system leading to higher levels of performance of the students and hence to more freedom in the new language. This chapter is devoted to as wide a use of the charts as is compatible with any group we might teach.

Although the examples chosen are limited to one set of charts because of the use of English in this writing, the reference to adaptations of this work to four other languages is provided in the Appendices.

Nine of the twelve English word charts seem to carry a sufficient functional vocabulary for the purpose of achieving what we described in the previous chapters. There is one way of increasing the number of the words referred to with the pointer and that is to make the students agree that, by leaving parts of words and their pronunciation (via color) as they appear on the charts and making one change in the appearance, a word existing in the language can be generated. Thus *hold* can become *sold* by covering the *h* and pointing at an *s; read* can become *dead* or *head* by similar means; *keep* can become *peep*. Substitution, subtraction, addition, insertion, reversal are all capable of being used easily to increase the vocabulary reachable on the charts. Of course, *-ly, -ing, -er,* and *-est* have already widened the set and have been used when the original vocabulary on the charts was being unfolded.

Now we want to increase the outcome from the actual words seen, and those we can easily make, using the method just mentioned, i.e., by involving students in statements or in insights that can be open to them but most likely would not come to them spontaneously.

We can, for instance, show that, as a question, many of the words can be used as a one word sentence: "what?" is obvious but "red?" or "his?" are as acceptable. So we play games making the students aware that: "here?" "one?" "them?" are indeed statements of the language being studied. Most of these words being on chart 1, this is a game we can start early if we so wish.

We then form systematically two, three, and four word sentences to show that more can be produced with the mastered vocabulary. For example, "end this!" or "his too?" can be illustrated by involving students in actions, the first with or without rods, the second with rods.

Since we cannot illustrate all possible sentences that can be formed, we shall only give a scattering of examples of the extensions of the use of vocabulary on the charts. Some are more telling than others, but familiarity with the charts will provide each teacher with many examples. Some are particularly useful; while others are unbelievably difficult to illustrate at this stage but can be put into circulation just the same to open people's eyes (and ears). Still others suggest later uses of the same materials, when the students are much more advanced than they may be when first shown these extensions.

Useful forms:

- *Possibly understandable at once, or easy to illustrate with rods:*

"Put it back there—give it a name—never!—so and so—name this place—never mind!—more and more—name that tune—evergreen—less and less—and what else—by oneself—more or less—forever and ever—whichever—whatever —whoever—whenever—wherever—right away of course!—right up—up and up—maybe— off she goes—nevertheless—they come in color and in black and white."

- *Colloquialisms which may be very difficult to illustrate with rods but may be included in classes with more advanced students and illustrated in various ways or verbally explained:*

"This is his take—give and take—I take this back—back him up—put this right—leave him to himself—leave me alone—put it in black and white—the more so—take them off my back—not all is black and white—to right a wrong—he wronged her—they hanged the wrong man—he saw red—red may mean left and left, red—he is from the left—what more?—never, ever—hardly ever—yours ever—and ever after—he made it—who is who—a self made man—what is there in a name?—by and by—by the way—by way of—in the red—in the black—off course—I am off—I am on—he is in the know—a knowhow—he put me on—one up—hold up—hard up—up and down—to stand on one's right—what can one do?"

7 Exploiting the Functional Vocabulary

This selection shows how much more can be done with the charts than was suggested in the previous chapter when the rods led the way. To provide readers with a more systematic approach, we shall suggest twelve exercises that can be done in part in the classroom (and when mini charts are available* also at home if students try their hand on their own). These exercises will follow the introduction of twelve charts one after the other for most languages, each new set showing what happens when one more chart is made available to the students. One of the meanings of these words can be introduced using rods as described in the previous chapter. In conjunction with this, a number of exercises will be proposed which readers may have wanted to know about but were not given up to this point. This chapter is stressing the enormous resources stored in the charts by showing a number of usages. There are others, and users may suggest more. But their number is sufficient to tell anyone what a mine has been put in the hands of teachers and students alike.

In this chapter readers will find illustrated in the case of the English language—what they can accumulate in any other language.**

Reviewing what had been done with the rods and charts as described in the previous chapters, teachers can generate a set of new awarenesses for their students.

---

* Now available only for ESL.

** For teachers of French, Italian, Spanish or Mandarin, the Appendices in this book will provide a progressive list of expressions that can be made in a manner similar to the one illustrated here.

For example, looking at the words on chart 1, the teacher says:

1. Can you write most of the statements we formed when we studied that chart in the lessons? Make your own list.

2. Make as long a statement as you can using only these words.

3. Reclassify the words on the chart putting together those that can replace each other. Do they have the same grammatical function? Can some words be placed in different sets? which? say why.

4. Expressions that can be used one for the other are called "equivalent." Write as many equivalent expressions as you can using only the words in this chart.

5. Give orders for pointing out sentences and watch whether they are executed properly. Follow up the execution with other orders to cancel the effect of the first when this is possible.

6. Form questions with words on the chart and whenever possible arrange them with corresponding answers into a kind of conversation.

These exercises can be extended as soon as we shift from the vocabulary of one chart to that contained in the first two charts, then the first three, and so on. It will be assumed that the readers see in the few words just written a number of active lessons involving the students in manners similar to those already met in previous chapters, but in exercises that take them beyond where they have been until then. The members of the class can be as involved as those actually called upon to point at words on the charts or to have a conversation which becomes easier as the words on more charts get included to extend the scope of the verbal intercourse.

Clearly sentences can be formed easily with the pointer on the charts regardless of whether they refer to the rods or not. But while it is somewhat easy for students to generate meaningful sentences relating to the rods once they have practiced a certain number of them, it is almost impossible for them to produce those statements which are made of these functional words and which come naturally to a native. We have divided our lists into three parts: we call A—those sentences or statements which can be guessed at, with some likelihood that the meaning will come through, such as "many of us are white;" B—those sentences or statements which offer a figurative meaning or are colloquialisms; and C—those sentences which show the expansion of power of the students in terms of length, complexity of grammar, and thought.

Here are the successive examples.

- *With Chart 1 alone:*

    A: "Back to back—are these his and hers?— here it is green and here it is black—these oranges are green not red—give these to them to give them to these—as it is, he is not black—take the whites, the yellows and the reds and give the browns, the blues and the yellows; these too are his."

B: "End it here!—take me—put an end to it—these white ones!—it's the blues—brown them—her back is red, his is brown and these two are a brownish orange—give one another one and to another one give one too."

C: He backs her—he gives them to her to brown—is the orange the one?—to these he too is two—he put these here and not the white ones—he led them back and two are here—the other one is red—as he is a red, brown, black, yellow and white are one.

- *With Charts 1 and 2*

    A: what's this?—as dark as black—I have got it for you—so and so got it—my light is out—he and I put it here—there are five here—there are none there

    B: which is which?—is this other another one?—take both of us—we are different!—got it?—me too!—and so what?—none too many— they name mine—I have her light and she mine—theirs are there and there's none too dark

    C: both are white and for both black is not a color—the two of them is not the same as both—you have got the same as both of us and it is for us and not for you—how can you sit right there and not take any of this as it is: it is for me and for none other.

Before moving on to what can be done with the words of Charts 3 to 12 when each one is added in turn, let us consider ways of teaching "advanced students" the material under A, B and C above.

By "advanced students" we mean those who have gone through the work covered in the preceding chapters and have at least one meaning for each of the words, the one met in conjunction with the rods.

A Sentences

Chart 1

"Back to back;" since we have met the meaning of that word in the statement easily concretized with the rods: "give them back to him or her," we now can point at the part of one's body and say "this is my back" and ask: "is this her back?" or "what is this?" and expect the answer "his or her back." Then invite two students to the front of the class and place them so that their position suggests to the other student: "X and Y are now back to back," later "they are no longer back to back; they are now side by side."

"Give these to them to give them to these" The teacher places two students at one end of the table and two at the other end and calls up another student to him; the order is given about rods on the table pointing at one pair when *them* is used and the other pair when *these* is said. He can then exchange the students so as to use one in his place or turn to the class and look at how they point at *these* and *them* alternately.

Charts 1 & 2
"Which is which?" after asking "what is this?" about each of a few rods and getting the answers by color, the teacher asks the above question to which the students would reply: "this one is blue, etc." Then placing a few objects that may have been labeled before (a box, a lid, a cup) on the table, after the labels have been given by the class in a sequence, some of the students ask *"which is which?"* of each other.

"My light is out;" light has been used to distinguish the two green rods, now it has a different meaning. A match can be lit and the teacher asks: "Do you have a cigarette for me?" If a student says "here it is" he can respond "light it for me" and before the student can do it he puts the match out and says "the light is out." (The word *out* is produced out of *our* in chart 2 be substituting *t* for *r*.) Then the teacher can go to the switch to put a light on without saying anything and turn it off, the class can be expected to say "the light is *out*" the teacher can say "or the light is *off* and now it is *on,* now off etc." In the case of gas lighters, "the flame or light will be on or out."

B Sentences

Chart 1
"Give another one to one and to another one, give one too;" we begin by having two students at the table and by putting to them the first part of the sentence "give another one to one" and when

this is executed properly asking two other students to the table and putting to them the content of the whole sentence.

For some of the other sentences it may be necessary to prepare material from magazines to illustrate the meanings as, for example, for the sentence: "Her back is red, his is brown and these two are a brownish orange" using cut out figurines and coloring them.

For "*Brown them,*" a toaster can convey the meaning at once.

Charts 1 & 2
"*And so what?*" the teacher calls four students to his table and arranges them in one way, then in another, then in a third, then in a fourth. After each he turns to the class and says nothing, then returns to make another arrangement. The class is perplexed. He encourages the students to say something and they do not know what to say. So he points at the words on the two charts and they read aloud: "and so what?"

"*Theirs are there and there's none too dark;*" the purpose of this example is to draw attention to, or to test awareness of *theirs* and *there's* and to show the two meanings of *there* as in "there is" and as in "put it there." The situation can be arranged with rods (which may indicate that the sentence belongs to the *A* group). As an A sentence the students have met "none is dark— this is too dark" and now they meet "none is too dark." Starting with "yours are here and theirs are there" the last segment is isolated and the sentence begins with these words but is not completed; "theirs are there . . . and none too dark," the students will see that they need a word to link the two segments. The teacher points at *there's* on the chart.

C Sentences

These exercises are for still more advanced students.

Chart 1

"As he is red, brown, black, yellow and white are one;" reading this sentence properly requires a pause after red, the recognition that red stands for leftist in politics and that the colors that follow are references to people of different races. At this level of work the teacher can count on addressing his class in English so that notions can be made clear.

The real test of understanding at this stage could be the production of sentences of increased complexity and length. The set given forces awareness that restriction upon a given vocabulary goes with inventiveness and, therefore, with freedom. If students can propose their own examples, it is not necessary to work on the one given here. Otherwise these can serve mainly to enhance awareness and parts of each can be treated as B-sentences.

For example with Chart 1 & 2: *"Both are white and for both black is not a color;"* the second part is needed to indicate that in the first part, "both" refers to people who must be white people and the reference to black not being a color—which is also a definition in physics—forces awareness that they must have transcended racial distinctions. It is the multiple levels of this use of speech that distinguishes students of a language from natives. Hence the reason for our placing these sentences at the C-level. It must not be expected that good users of the language can, without much reading of the literature, manage to produce sentences showing a functioning at all these levels simultaneously. It is an ambitious aim for teachers, one that has been shown here to be compatible with the vocabulary on the charts, but not one that results from it as do A-sentences or even B-sentences.

As an exercise for the readers, in what follows we have not separated the sentences in the three groups above, leaving to them the finding of the criteria that make a sentence one of three groups.

Charts 1, 2, 3
As soon as the words of Chart 3 are added, the explosion of power and opportunities is felt. The past tense that could only be made with *did* and *have* can now be made directly with *gave* and *took, left, told, taken* and *given*. The future tense with *will* and *shall*. A number of very useful words have appeared and now we can do a great deal more than before because of comparatives and superlatives while using what we learned from exercises 1 and 2.

> "So and so took it—it took you long for this—there are many that gave all they had—who is the one on the right?—for so long I told you that—from here to

there it is not short—can you tell him yes for that?—he left me right there—I have given her all I have—did she tell you that?—come! come! put an end to this—on what can you go?—he took very long to tell her not very much—I did like it but . . . —what was it that you got there?—who is it that took all those different cans?" and so on.

Charts 1-4

"Besides I did not like her very much because she took longer than anyone—he comes in under a different name and tells us it is his true name—between you and me they did not like how I speak—she looks so tall between those two short ones and side by side with them—in front there was less than behind and we put it all there—to top it all he put her down on the low side in front of us—would you show me how high you can put this?—like all of them he should come here first and go there last—they go first together as high as they can then one by one to the lowest mine—underneath it all there was a set of colored tops for all of us to take."

Charts 1-5

"Most of us did not like to pick on her—apart from telling them to go away we could not say much—the last one to ask for it was so old that he could not hold it as it was given him— enough is enough—everyone of us could hold a pick and hit hard on the lid—she is neither old nor young—everywhere I go I ask where am I? but also who am I?—after speaking with him I left for good—as much as I would like to I shall not say yes—they are up there, holding up on top of the trees—again and again I told him to shut up but he goes on speaking all the time—what is new is that he likes to show up every few days."

Charts 1-6

"Did you hear the news?—is it good news?— listen to me, tell her that you have had enough of it—why did she go twice with him and not with me?—they threw a few at him and a few at her—there goes the first!—when I heard them speak, I gave thanks for how well I can speak— towards the end we asked why the light went out—thus far I could not see why we all did it so well—they can count on me but not I on them—when I asked, will you answer me, she said, maybe—well done, said he—I took a look and I did not like at all what I saw—did he throw it across once or twice?—what good will it do?— to hear I listen but does one hear to listen?—as shown on this, no one has heard of it before— after all he is so near her that he can say what she tells him to say—thanks a lot."

Charts 1-7

"We held exactly two close to each other—I am looking forward to your coming to see us— weight is what makes things heavy—can one make quiet as one makes noise?—my being so loud is not so good for me—all this falls within his hold—what is wrong with this?—this is the wrong one—it will do—do it as I say—he is so slow—slow down, will you?—above all because they are close they see everything in the same way—you stand up quickly, you move fast, you tell us slowly what you saw there— someone is holding up—somewhere here there is someone whose name is English—to begin with I would like to say . . . —some begin where others leave off—exactly what is it you want to say?—I measured it exactly and stand by my answer—must you do it this way?"

Charts 1-8

"I know that you know—I know that you know that I know—1 know that you know that I know that you know—1 know that you know that I know that you know that I know—he knew it was impossible—I spoke to him softly but firmly—in addition to speaking loud, he spoke as no one must speak on such occasions—I sat up and listened to all she had to say—he threw up—and this was thrown in in addition—he made it—she is off—they are off-putting— at least he is now used to it—sure I own it all— do not touch me; you do not know me—he has been below weight for a long time—and your next move?—the first touchdown is his—we expect zero from this—although I brought all the possible things thrown off from there, I was able at least to save about most of it—what a standoffish!—size him up first and then give him what he can take—from although we can make almost."

Charts 1-9

"However old I am I keep learning—may I write even if I spell wrongly?—always is the opposite of never—women buy what they must, and more—hardly ever—he chose four women whose age he did not know and could not tell which was the youngest or the oldest—since when is once equal to never?—unless they kept it open they could not see outside—she was anxious he might pick it up rather than drop it—let us be open and all will be well among us—when the car stopped he was thrown forward fast—women do not keep it all to themselves—as they came they went—he made the impossible possible—through it all he chose to shut up—ever since he learned to spell well he does not stop to write—unless he had read it, how would he know about this?"

Charts 1-10

"One thousand million light years is not impossible in the cosmos—six of one, and half dozen of the other—fifty fifty—thanks a million —is ninety years old enough?—so young at eighty—he has a million and is so mean—how many times is this bigger than that?—she is a teenager."

Charts 1-11

"The twelfth night—Friday the thirteenth—the longest day—April fool's—Ash Wednesday— the date of today—today I have a date—the year round—Good Friday—a leap year—a lean year—a fat year—monthly news—twice yearly —eighth in succession—Easter day—the twenty fifth of December—the Ides of March— week after week after week—mid-week is Wednesday or Thursday—thirty or thirty one days form one month, except February which normally has twenty eight days—when February has twenty nine days, the year is called a leap year; once every four years there is a leap year."

Charts 1-12

"Wait a minute—soon it will be seven o'clock —long ago or once upon a time do not tell when it was—just a moment—one fourth is another name for one quarter—soon means in a few moments—noon or midday means twelve o'clock—evening comes earlier in winter than in summer—if today is the present then tomorrow is the future and yesterday the past— summer time is also called daylight saving time —half an hour is also thirty minutes or eighteen hundred seconds—while I looked at the spring, those present went out to come back an hour later to tell me that as it was evening I could not see very much, but all that time I saw so many new things that not even midsummer night dreams could begin to compare—I often thought that until that moment at which the future becomes the past no present can come forward—yet I would ask, how much more this world would be good for us if we knew how to look after our own selves and see to it that everything be kept well and in its place."

The considerable number of sentences indicated above represent a small fraction of what can be done with the functional vocabulary. Teachers will know that they have indeed learned to use the instrument of the word charts when they can feel the statement above to be a fact every time they look at the charts. Both they and their classes will know something very valuable about language in general and the language they are studying in particular. We already mentioned the role of triggers that words play and the converse, which is that thought can be couched in words once we know what we think as well as how to express ourselves. Our students may not have to be taught to think as much as to express themselves precisely, concisely and adequately. To this end the work of this chapter can be considered essential.

8 Reading and Writing in the New Language

Our students have been looking at charts from almost the beginning, therefore words in any language are perceptible items for them and we can spend some time to make them copy the designs. When there are rules like those for Chinese, Hindi and Arabic, we can teach them in one lesson the strokes which have been invented to help in designing the characters for legibility and aesthetics.

But even if we do not pay special attention to calligraphy, practice will both improve legibility in speed writing and recognition of signs.

Initially, reading will mean the sounding of the words on the charts as well as the sentences formed with the pointer on the words of the charts. As soon as these words are transferred to a chalkboard using, say, white chalk or to paper using a pen or pencil, the activity of looking at the sequence in order to utter it, will obviously become reading. Exchanging the papers among the students will generate the opportunity for students to recognize designs produced by other writers.

Also at the beginning, it is the teacher who points at sentences while the students only put them down. They can fill pages with these sentences, and this activity can be varied as follows: first the sentences are very short and read in chorus by the students and only then put down on paper, later the sentences get longer and are not read until they have been put down. Students listen to some reading them, following word by word on their rendition, and comment on the reading, correcting or passing, accordingly. A student could be handed the pointer and at the same time as others read, or before or after, point at the sentence on the charts. As the sentences become longer and longer, the students prove that they can hold them in their mind and pull them out in the required order and form them on paper, observing the structure of the statement.

Another exercise will be to let the students look at the words on the charts and form their own sentences. In the beginning they will be shy and produce mainly slight variations on the sentences already met, but if the teacher urges them to try what has not been seen, some students may dare to propose a statement of his or her own.

If this opportunity occurs then 1) either the statement is correct and can serve as a basis for the variations it offers, or 2) it can be put right by a small alteration either in the words or in their

8 Reading and Writing in the New Language

order and produces the occasion to widen the scope of the exercise, or 3) it is awfully wrong and too complicated to put right. In this latter case the teacher simply suggests dropping the exercise and hopes that soon it will be possible to cope with the challenge when more of the language is available to generate a feel for its quality.

For beginners the addition of a new chart represents, as we saw in Chapter 6, an explosion which makes many more sentences possible. Of these only a few will have been selected in the class work involving the teacher. Therefore, when the teacher invites the students to make their own choices, a number of new statements might be produced. While it is possible to let students 1) read aloud what they have written (with or without someone else pointing to the words on the charts), or 2) exchange their papers and either ask questions about what they see or comment on the statements or even suggest corrections, the teacher can also glean sentences from among those produced and reproduce them as reading material for the next lesson.

In such cases the vocabulary will be known since the words have been selected from the charts, and it is part of the lessons as devised in earlier chapters to make sure that students pay their ogdens in terms of sounds, stresses and meaning. So what the statements are displaying is the contact with the structures of the language possible with such a vocabulary. The fact that students will always be looking at what they are already familiar with will permit the teacher to work on the flow of words so as to make it sound like that of natives in the phrasing and the melody.

Clearly this process can be extended as charts are added one after another to the display and as the vocabulary has been acquired, via work on the rods and with the rods. We can therefore expect that there will be an increase in the length and complexity of statements, in the variety of what they refer to, thus displaying greater autonomy on the part of the students and giving the teacher a choice of statements to work on, either in order to put right some of the forms offered by the students, or in order to widen the scope of the classroom book of sentences stamped with the personality and idiosyncrasies of a particular class.

As we reach the end of the set of charts and most of the functional vocabulary has been integrated (i.e., with ogdens paid and practice given) we shall have in the classes advanced beginners and what we can do with them now will apply also to intermediate students, that is, to a course for people who claim that they do not need to go through the set exercises above and those in Chapter 6.

Reading thus far has entailed familiarization with the script, the spellings of the words looked at, and the production of statements with a restricted functional vocabulary buttressed by writing of the same. When students receive the sheets teachers have prepared from their students' own statements, they begin reading what slowly becomes a book.

The gradation of statements found in such a book displays the actual progress of the students and is by construction always at the level of the class. Comprehension has been built-in and this will ease the problems of being able to read this material as well as natives.

The extension of reading will be concomitant with 1) the extension of writing as ten wall pictures are introduced and the vocabulary is expanded (cf. Chapter 9), and 2) the introduction of the three books that are part of The Silent Way materials: "A Thousand Sentences," "Short Passages" and "Eight Tales" (cf. Chapter 10).

In Chapter 7 and the Appendices, we have shown how the use of the charts can be extended to include colloquialisms and the expressions that only use the functional vocabulary and the shaded meanings associated with these words.

There is a level of reading, we have called R_4, that is concerned with extracting new knowledge from a text. (The reading we have considered so far has extended over R_1-R_3* and did not raise the problem of using the new language as an instrument of study and for acquiring information.) R_4 presents itself, for example, when foreign students attend school and college outside their own countries and need to take courses and sit for competitive or other examinations in the new language. This kind of reading utilizes those we have worked on earlier. But since words have no meaning of their own, texts can only deliver their contents if students either have a dictionary to obtain definitions of words not yet met, or only meet sentences that are definitions (which occurs very rarely), or translate their texts

---

* A notation explained in our reading program "Words in Color."

into their own language. To prepare people for R_4, we must enter upon special exercises which, if they have been given to the students chronologically, would come after the experience acquired via the techniques of the next two chapters.

The reading of newspapers or magazines makes demands which entitle it to be labeled R_4, except that in general there is no test of what one has retained from such reading.

In classes it is possible to use—after the work with rods and the charts has been thoroughly gone through—chosen articles of newspapers which offer sentences that do not contain an accumulation of nouns and adjectives that are part of a specialized vocabulary. It may happen that hunting for articles exemplifying such situations will yield a collection of texts easily accessible after the work mentioned above has been completed. Sometimes appended drawings or cutouts from magazines and catalogues may be sufficient to produce an illustrated text that yields as much meaning to the students as it does to natives.

The variety of subject matter in a national daily or weekly paper is enormous and may be sufficient to widen one's vocabulary in those fields. Although the approach may not be as systematic and complete as it is in "A Thousand Sentences," it clearly refers to everyday life subjects that, particularly in the case of adults, may meet their interests and represent sufficient motivation for reading.

Exercises can be associated with the articles read: paraphrasing paragraphs; giving definitions for some words; making a precis of what was read; commenting on the content; answering questions put by the teacher on some aspects of the topic or that challenge the depth of comprehension. One exercise which could be attempted, when circumstances permit, is to request an impromptu translation in the student's language (if it is understood by the teacher).

Translation is a companion of reading and writing. Throughout our oral work with the rods and the visual dictation on the charts, we have carefully avoided the use of the students' native languages. We have even succeeded in blocking them so that the students relate to the new language directly and as a particular set of challenges. Generally we succeed well in that task because of our silence as teachers and the students' struggle to utter every word. Sometimes students deeply involved in such a learning do not even notice when their teacher is using their own language.

Now we are suggesting that students use their mother tongue to produce expressions equivalent to what they can say in the new language, that they write these down and discover that they have two languages at their disposal for the same functions, this will allow them to increase the population they can relate to, perhaps vastly. Translation is here not for learning a language but for testing one's knowledge of one language recently acquired against one which is already second nature.

It would be helpful to suggest exercises to make translation a two-way traffic. For example, suppose a situation with the rods is proposed: this can trigger statements in two languages. Then instead of a situation, the students can be given the corresponding statement from which to produce either first the situation with the rods and then their statement in their own language, or the other way round. Thus statements and reality will be interchangeable in the mind of the translator. This is the ordinary state of mind of professional translators. Reading and writing have, consequently, merged in a number of ways.

In the teaching of languages, reading is often considered as the aim of learning the language, as it seems capable of opening through their literature the culture of the people who habitually speak that language. Here we have considered that reading has several meanings and worked on a number of them. The following chapters add some others contributions to this study.

9 Expansion of Vocabulary

The work on reading and writing in Chapter 8 was connected primarily with what can be done with the rods and the charts.

Although the rods can be used to symbolize entities other than themselves: such as numerals, construction bricks, lines of plans of rooms, houses, streets, parks and even human beings, acting as puppets on the table, moved by the teacher's hands (while he speaks about what he intends to suggest by this manipulation) it may be very difficult to do with them what is so easy to do with drawings and pictures.

Therefore, the introduction of pictures suggests itself for consideration. The choice of what to present students in their case is unlimited and in The Silent Way our choice is based on common sense, which dictates that we restrict ourselves in a way we have found useful so far by proposing: 1) a focal point that gathers the students' attention, 2) means that already trigger words in one's own language and that serve as supporters for words in the new language, 3) a controlled situation that evokes a certain number of desirable words and expressions, 4) images that help to ease the retention of clusters of words.

If we want students to be free in the field of expanded vocabularies as well as in the previous phases, clearly we must maintain the same kind of triggering of language by perception as we had before. If we want students to be free from distractions we must 1) give them a schematized situation that does not take their minds away by making them dream, 2) limit ourselves to everyday language by including only those details that refer to it and leaving out what is specialized, 3) keep the situation open to the imagination so the teacher can select a number of possible entries into statements that are supported by the flexibility of details in the picture. The latter will let students experience that their perception and their imagination can go hand in hand in making them better users of the functional language mixed with the new vocabulary.

In order to make the use of pictures as flexible as we would like, we have associated a four-page worksheet with each of them. On page 1 we have reproduced in black and white the picture the worksheet refers to. On page 2 we give a number of words which refer to the picture, although this is not so specified. Requests are made (in print in the new language) to classify these words by affinity (i.e., by reference to the meanings associated by natives to these words and properties of these items that can make them be conceived as belonging to some classes; cf., below). On page 3 we give additional words and ask students to produce statements involving these words, those found on page 2, and the functional vocabulary. Page 4 is a blank one for

9 Expansion of Vocabulary

writing a "composition" in the new language on what the picture triggers in the individual student.

Clearly page 1 can be used to indicate which labels can be written to refer to each item recognizable on the picture as having an associated word in the new language. But in order to continue our support of our students, so that they feel independent and maintain their autonomy in this phase of the work, this is what we do.

After hanging a classroom picture on the chalkboard, the teacher points to an item on it and either tells the students loudly and clearly the label associated with it, or writes it legibly and asks for it to be read by one student or by the class in chorus. This is repeated for all the items the teacher decides are of significance for this class. Then, pointing to the written words at random, the teacher asks the student to read them and follows that by pointing to the item itself and asking for its name. In some classes a further exercise can be offered, students are called to the chalkboard and the teacher, or a student appointed by him, utters one of the words. This is pointed at and immediately afterwards the corresponding item on the picture. Judgment of correctness is left to the class. Once this further familiarization has taken place, the teacher thoroughly erases the collection of words and asks the students to look at page one of the worksheet and to write in pencil the labels triggered by the items on it.

This exercise may take a few minutes and then the teacher can ask students to pair up, swap worksheets, and examine together the set of words they have produced for exactitude and spelling.

They can suggest to each other the changes they think are needed, and these, if they are acceptable, can be put by the original writer on his worksheet.

Following this, a further step is taken: asking the class to restore on the chalkboard the designs of the labels that the teacher had written at first. Comparison of this with what is on page 1 of the worksheet will tell each student how much he or she can count on his or her payment of ogdens for the retention of the labels.

An alternative to this exercise is to have pairs of students use page 2 of one of their worksheets to check the spelling of the words written around the picture on page 1 of the other's worksheet. This comparison does not ensure the correctness of the labeling of the items; only a good memorization does (or a real payment of ogdens).

Page 2 of the worksheets has thus been found to contain words in the new language which refer to items in the picture. Its use for the question put at the top of it is either casually postponed to the following lesson (if no homework is given) or considered at home away from the picture when one is only looking at the words to find when and if they trigger an image to give their individual meaning. It is this set of meanings as well as the understanding of the instructions on the top line of page 2 that leads to the exercise which follows.

Given words are to be re-written in groups according to attributes of the reality they evoke. We call this principle of classification "affinity," which needs to be explained. Returning

9 Expansion of Vocabulary

to the picture studied and pointing to items on it, the teacher can say: "This and that go together, or belong together, or are in the same class, or are in the same group, or have an affinity," and write them in one column, asking the class for a third item to place in that column according to its label, because the item considered indeed belongs in some way to the class. Passing to an item which clearly does not belong in the class should lead students to start another column which can then be filled in with other items. After this (or if need be adding a third column) the rules for exercises on page 2 will be clearly understood for subsequent worksheets.

It is clear that there is no absolute order either in the choice of which picture and worksheet to take on or which word to choose on page 2 to begin the various classifications the words suggest. This allows students and teachers to adapt their choices according to their mood and to their judgment of the class level and state of mind, thus adding a minor element of flexibility to the approach.

Page 3 of each worksheet is concerned with a triple integration of 1) the language acquired thus far through rods and word charts, i.e., the structure of the language and the functional vocabulary, 2) the vocabulary of page 2, and 3) a new set of words on page 3 which are mainly qualifiers of what the picture suggests.

This page is devoted to the free writing of sentences triggered by the situation described here as a triple integration. The sentences do not need to be related to one another, although no one is asking them to be kept as independent statements either.

The work on page 3 is individual and can be done at school or at home, or started in one place and finished in the other. Its main contribution is to make students aware of their capacity to use new vocabulary at once in meaningful statements of which the words are the only visible component (that is, the imagery in their mind remains unseen to all but themselves). A freer level of expression is thus reached and can aim toward responsible communication.

Of course, the teacher can seize the opportunity of the presentation of spontaneous written statements (hence more permanent) by the students to find out how much of the language is at their disposal, which structures are still shaky, which activities were not sufficient to make students note spellings, use structures, and revise their renderings. Group work can follow when the most promising sentences are taken from the worksheets and put on the chalkboard for examination by all. This may mean that a particular statement is a model for correctness or for brevity, or for aptness, or for melody etc., on the positive side, or an object for criticism by the class as far as the order of words, their spelling, the choice of expressions, the adequacy of each expression to its purpose etc., are concerned, for further work on improvement. Again group work is done on the material suggested by individual contributions.

Page 4 of the worksheet is the most ambitious step of all. The sheet is blank except for the instructions at the top, which asks for a composition produced entirely by the individual student who lets the picture tell him a story.

Page 4 tells of our optimism in this approach. We believe: 1) that students will attempt free composition at this stage (which may be, say, twenty hours after we've started teaching these students from scratch in the new language) and often we are not disappointed and 2) that students are equipped to try this sort of thing out and gain from it a precious feedback about themselves as learners of this language and as users of themselves with respect to this material.

Page 4, therefore, is a useful achievement test for those who dare attack it at the stage suggested to them that they take it. It will not say much that is useful, though, to those who do not attempt it, for until they do we only know that they do not feel like exposing themselves.

In fact, each worksheet is an individual multiple test which gives us opportunities to learn about teaching, about the approach, and about how to trust students while individualizing the way we meet them and make them work.

Some of the page 3 sentences and page 4 compositions can be gathered to broaden the class book for reading and mentioned in the previous chapter. Students' productions can be vital material because of the originality shown by the unpredictable writers involved in the project.

The above tells of the worksheets concerning the 10 pictures we produced for the benefit of the students. Now we shall talk about the pictures themselves, and the way we have thought of using them in the classroom. The numbers given to the pictures do not describe an order except, perhaps that #1 is not as susceptible as the others to yielding a very large vocabulary.

There could have been many more pictures than ten, but we stopped at this number since other means suggested themselves to take students beyond these stages, while generating variety and openings towards larger horizons.

#1 THE CAT

Vocabulary, 1) for the background: *a wall, floor, door, baseboard, shadow, light* or *sunlight*; 2) for the animal itself: *head, ears, whiskers, neck, back, fur, tail, paws (hind and front)*, 3) for the mood: *attentive, cautious, on his guard*, 4) for some verbs: *stands, pushes, walks, lights up, casts shadows*.

9 *Expansion of Vocabulary*

#2 THE BEDROOM

Vocabulary, 1) besides walls, floor — words already met — the words for the room itself include: *ceiling, window, curtains, carpet, bed, bedside table, wall picture and frame, armchair,* 2) for a person's living: *slippers, pajamas, ashtray, bedding* (*pillow, pillow case, sheet, blanket, eiderdown*); for the bed: *head of, foot of, mattress, legs;* for the armchair: *back, arms, legs.*

#3 THE MAN

Vocabulary, 1) for the setting: *at home, casual, sitting down, holding, vacation, unemployed, rest, interested, concentrating, read, smiling, holidays;* 2) for the man: *lap, leg, crossed, hand, forehead, elbow, wrist, shoulder, teeth, brow, nose, face, hips, ankle, knee, finger, neck, mouth, nail, thumb,* 3) for the clothing: *trousers, buttonhole, socks, shirt, collar, sleeve, slacks, button,* 4) for objects: *pipe, glasses, seat, newspaper, crossword puzzle, rockers, rocking chair,*

#4 THE PICNIC

Vocabulary, 1) for going on a picnic: *meal, snack, friend, appetite, park, on the way, simple, carry, inviting, hungry, go out, disposable, trunk:* 2) for the setting: *tree, branches, shady, grass, basket, leaves, blade, summer dress, boy, sleeveless, leaning, offers, youth, sandals;* 3) for things to bring: *napkin, bottle, plate, cork, knife, cloth, glass;* 4) for things to *eat: food, bananas, apples, drink, bread, sausage, fruit, sandwich, cheese.*

9 *Expansion of Vocabulary*

#5 THE HOUSE

Vocabulary, 1) for the house: *roof, chimney, tiles, gutters, attic, front door, windows, shut, story, garage, step, dwelling, home;* 2) for the yard: *back yard, shrubs, lawn, hedge, flowers, path, flowerbed, low wall, gate, garden, cared for;* 3) for the surroundings: *sidewalk, mailbox, curb pavement, traffic, street, concrete, silent, neighborhood, the suburbs, in the city, quiet, child, toddler, people, fine weather, rain.*

#6 A SCENE

Vocabulary, 1) for the people and their activities: *girl, daughter, mother, lesson, practice, play, worry, worried, excited, chase, warn;* 2) for the room: *panes, frame, glass, stool, score, piano keys, ivory, handles, lid, wall hangings, indoors, living room, closed;* 3) for the setting: *temperature, spring, outdoors, foliage, season, morning, soil, earth, dog, play, worry, worried, excited, chase, warn.*

#7 THE CAR

9 Expansion of Vocabulary

Vocabulary, 1) for the car itself: *steering wheel, hood, engine, spokes, tires, fender, rear-view mirror, headlight, windshield wipers, license plate, brakes, odometer, gearshift, wheels, turn signals, parking lights, speedometer;* 2) for life on the road: *driving, fast, speed, trip, roads, corner, skid, ride, driver, pedestrian, passenger;* 3) for driving a luxury car: *elegant, well-built, expensive, status, rich, classic, model.*

#8 THE FAMILY

Vocabulary, 1) for people in the family: *father, grandmother, boy, son, family, brother, sister, alike, parents, grandparents, children, offspring, relatives,* 2) for things to wear: *hat, jacket, sweater, vest, tie, shorts, pants, dress, stockings, gloves, coat, belt, bow, blouse, ribbon;* 3) for going out: *leisure time, enjoying themselves, visit, afternoon, bus stop, church, makeup, middle class, dressed up, Sunday:* 4) for things to carry: *cane, pocketbook, mirror, comb, handbag, kite, pocket, wallet.*

#9 THE SUPERMARKET

Vocabulary, 1) for going shopping: *choose, buy, examine, discount, consider, errand, shopping bag, special, enjoy, look, list, bonus, bargain, sale, customer, wait;* 2) for in the shop: *store clerk, counter, shop window, stacked up, weigh, compartment, cashier, aisle, computerized scales, freezer, shelf, rack, container, jar, cans, package;* 3) for things to buy: *cauliflower, butter, cheese, dairy products, yogurt, meat, tea, coffee, sugar, jam, candy, rolls, cookies, jelly, beer, oil, grapes, ham, vegetables, fruit juice, soda, soups, onions, celery, cabbage, pears, ice, grapefruit, produce, groceries, milk, frozen foods.*

#10 THE RESTAURANT

Vocabulary, 1) for setting the table: *place settings, knife fork, napkin, bottle, carafe, pot, salt shaker, plate, breadbasket, butter dish, tablecloth, silverware, spoon, pitcher, set;* 2) for going to the restaurant: *menu, announcement, sign, regular customer, waitress, owner, place, party, reservation, special occasion, personnel, specialty, guest, tip, date, sitting arrangements,* 3) for other vocabulary connected with eating and eating habits: *wine, mustard, water, noon, meal, supper, dinner, lunch, breakfast, drinks, softdrinks.*

Treatment of one of the Pictures as an Example: the Family

The treatment follows the outline given in the beginning of this chapter. The vocabulary around the picture will form at least two rings and the number of arrows may create confusion. Hence the choice has to be made of which words should be presented first, practiced thoroughly and then erased before the second and then a third set of words is introduced.

Say we choose names first: *Dad, Mr. Smith,* and *Mom, Mrs. Smith; sons: Peter, John, Ken* (any names will do); *daughters: Jennie, Emily.* We then engage the class in describing the scene by saying what they see: "The *whole* family is standing in one *row.*" (The words in italics may have to be supplied by the teacher, and form the second set of words). "Dad and Mom are in the middle, their sons are on their right and their daughters on their left.—Mom holds Ken's Hand, Peter holds a *model airplane* while John has a *kite* in his right hand that Ken wants to take from him.—Mom is holding him back.—Jennie looks at herself in a small *mirror* while Emily ties her *purse*. Both have *gloves* in their left hand. Jennie is *combing* her hair with her right hand holding a comb in it. The two *girls* have *ribbons* in their hair. Jennie uses hers to hold her *pigtail* in a *bow,* Emily has a *band* over her head.—Dad has a three-piece *suit,* his *jacket* has three buttons, he has a *tie,* a *pocket handkerchief* and holds in his hands his *hat* and his *cane* (or *stick*). Under his jacket is his *vest.*—Mom holds her *pocketbook* in her left hand against her *breast.*—Ken is the only one with a *coat.*—Do all the children have *sweaters* on?—They all wear *shoes.*—Mom has on high *heels.*—On Mom's hat there are *feathers.*"

A third set of words can be introduced and used immediately in sentences. "Peter and John have shoes with *laces;* Ken's shoes have *buckles;* Emily's one button each. The others have easy shoes.—The girls and Ken wear knee socks. John's socks are doubled at the knee.—Of the three boys only Peter has long *trousers* like his dad. Jennie has a pleated *skirt.*—Dad is *bald* and looks at Jennie affectionately.—All seem very *busy* with one thing or another.—This is perhaps a *middle-class* family or it is a special occasion for going out as a family.—They may be waiting for a *bus* on the *sidewalk.*— They do not seem to be *in a hurry.*—Since people do not take toys to *church,* we may say that the family is perhaps going out on a *visit* or just out to *a park.*—Ken's hair is *parted* on the left, Peter's on the right. John has a *crew-cut* hair style.—Mom and Dad look *old-fashioned* with *conventional dressing habits* of how to be dressed and how to dress their children.—It may be *mid-fall* or *mid-spring* since only Mom has an *overcoat.*—The *forecast* is for no *rain* since no

9 Expansion of Vocabulary

one has an *umbrella*.—Mom's pocketbook is rather *bulky* and may contain lots of things. The girls' pocketbooks are tiny and possibly empty.—They are not all standing on one *plane* as we can see that Mom is partly covered by Dad. There could be three planes with the girls in front, Dad slightly behind them and the other four still behind in one plane with Mom.—It is not clear from the picture that all these children are *brothers* and *sisters*. Some of them may be *adopted* children. Perhaps even Mr. and Mrs. Smith are not their *parents* at all. They may be *guardians* taking their *charges* on an *outing*."

With these final statements we are entering the free composition phase connected with page 4 of the worksheet, while the sentences formed could well be written on page 3. Of course, the words for "the youngest child, the oldest ones, the middle children" are all part of what can be done with the charts and are not luxury vocabulary even if used for the first time on the occasion of this exercise. The teacher may note how his or her class does the work above and decide either to give part of a story suggested by the picture (for page 4 of the worksheet) or to collect individual statements to form the classroom work to be studied by all.

The flexibility we encourage should be visible here too. Reading compositions will be added to all previous reading, and this material can serve to show how important the functional vocabulary is when we get involved in acquiring a language as a set of structures that display the spirit of the people who inherit it. But for the expansion of vocabulary the payment of ogdens is needed, and this we do via the instrument of the book "A Thousand Sentences."

A Thousand Sentences

It is obvious that a book in any one language does not reveal its secret even to someone who can decode each word. Words are not symbols: they do not say much by themselves as symbols do. They are merely signs, essentially arbitrary but showing our intelligence some clues through something of their form. This is why we can develop a process of cracking statements open even when we do not have immediate access to them. For instance, prefixes, suffixes, roots, or stems suggest probable meanings. Consistency between the words in one sentence or between sentences in one paragraph may yield to our intelligence, coupled with retention, some idea of what the text in question is about.

Hence reading a book in any one language is a hazardous but not altogether impossible task. Still, books can only be looked at after one is well experienced in a language.

That is why we introduce our first book only now and do not resort to any artifact besides the written word to propose the next dramatic expansion of our power in the meeting of the new language.

Newcomers to a language must be given tasks they can relate to, not so difficult as to discourage nor so easy as to appear trivial. We considered the device "of presenting the hurdles of reading texts reduced each to one sentence," leaving the connection between them generally very loose. Hence we can embark in reading amounts restricted to one sentence only, if that is considered the contribution of this book in any one particular lesson. This flexibility is important at this stage for it tells students that the task of reading is not the accumulation of pages turned but the many things that can be done with one sentence, some of them, or many of them.

The book is organized so as to be concerned with words used in the various aspects of everyday life, beginning with one's place of dwelling and moving further and further away in space, time and complexity. A look at the table of contents will show this. But what is not visible is that we can use the sentences for a number of functions that would help students to be freer and to expand their command of the language.

Since the level at which the book is introduced is known in advance, we already know that students understand that phrasing and intonation are needed and contribute to comprehension. We give students sentences to read but do not yet ask for an understanding of content since there are words that trigger no meaning in each of them. Reading *as if* one understood is one of the exercises we give our students in order to make sure that the words are not read in isolation, that the appearance of a question mark, an exclamation mark, a comma, a colon, a semi-colon, a full stop, generates in the reader behaviors recognizable by what the voice does or by the duration of a pause. If phrasing is still shaky, it is possible to associate to each sentence a set of figures describing what is required. For example 3-3-2-1-5-3-3-2-4 tells the student that the following sentence must be read as:

"This is partly/because of climate/and partly/because/different parts of the country/ have been influenced/by the customs/that foreigners/have brought with them/."

In addition the teacher can use his hands to indicate by lifting or holding horizontally or moving down that the sentence requires the voice to be raised, to be kept steady or to be brought down. Drawing on the chalkboard to provide a more visible instruction will produce something like:

A dozen or so sentences should establish the awareness that reading aloud resembles speaking and, therefore, can put at the disposal of the reader all that has been acquired so far in the oral work done with the rods and the charts. Students will become aware that some words are invariably run together in reading although they are separated in writing or print, that phrases can involve 1, 2 or 3 words very rarely more than 5. They will watch how the voice rises and falls and how the new language differs in melody from their own beyond its having some new sounds.

The above exercise can of course be done on any sentence found anywhere. But with this book, the isolation of sentences, which are numbered separately suggests this exercise as a first one and it happens to be an important one serving the speaker and the reader in every student.

Another exercise will consist in illustrating sentences or groups of sentences. Students are given catalogues of direct mail firms or advertising pages of newspapers showing objects mentioned in some of the sentences selected when studying objects in the home (crockery, silver, furniture, kitchen, bathroom, cleaning instruments) or in offices; pictures of musical instruments, bands and orchestras etc. Tables or plans can be made to indicate family relations, ranks in the forces, levels of administrations, structures in hierarchies in the churches, education, unions, etc. These clusters of words may be within or beyond the needs or interests of the particular class at work and teachers will have to select which sections of the book to leave out and which to illustrate.

"Stereotyped" compositions can be proposed to cluster some of the words. That means that a number of the sentences in this book can be thought of as describing one of the many social situations offered in them. For example, to cluster the labels given to the relationships of a family, students can write: "When a man who was married loses his wife by death, he is called a *widower,* but he is called a *divorcee* if she separates from him legally, or *abandoned* if she runs away. When husband and wife have no children of their own they can either *adopt* children or become *foster* parents according to the laws of their country," and so on.

The vocabulary given in "A Thousand Sentences" lends itself to such re-arrangement of statements to produce a continuous text for reading in the class. Teachers could give various students the task of producing compositions where sentences, in principle separated from each other, become the elements of a composition, if not a story.

But stories too can be attempted and may even turn out to be an easy and enjoyable task for some students who have a good command of the functional language and only need their imagination stirred by the contact with words and definitions found in these sentences. If teachers allow students to leave gaps for the words they wished they knew—but do not—to use along with other words that are available and, after the writing is handed back with the gaps filled by the teacher, we may discover a new instrument to measure learning within the freedom of doing the best one can with what one has.

It is clear that when teachers know what this book contains, they may be able to use in conjunction the 10 pictures and "A Thousand Sentences." In particular, the bedroom, the car on the road, the family and the supermarket can be found to provide images for words in some of the sections of the book. Students could be invited to suggest their own pictures for a set of sentences and, if these pictures could be made by someone in the class, they would well serve as those in the other materials did to cluster vocabularies and ease retention of non-functional words.

In this chapter we have taken cautious steps to expand the vocabulary beyond the functional. We may have reached a very respectable inventory of several thousand useful words and still no list of words has been memorized. To acquire the use of these words, the facility that is sign of mastery, we have proposed a few exercises that stress the notion of clustering. Of course, there are others. Conversation about the contents of any one of the pictures; the compositions on page 4 of the worksheets that can be extended to include a whole sequence of sentences of the book of sentences; free composition and free dialogues which can follow exercises as those suggested in the extension of the use of the wall charts in Chapter 7, all these will make students want to resort to wider and wider vocabularies to express themselves. Such needs will serve as a motivation to retain the words met in the lessons and in the homework.

10 Evaluating Progress

In all the exercises we engaged in, it was possible to keep our finger on the pulse of the learners. This chapter will be given to a close examination of the way we take care of being thoroughly informed of what goes on during the lessons and guided in our teaching by the input of the students.

Knowing that there are elements that students cannot invent, we cannot expect them to use these until they have managed to own them by retaining them—we say by paying their ogdens for them. Hence, in order to make sure that the students pay them, we, as teachers, must see to it that the element or elements in question are being related to properly. For example if it is a sound, that it is heard and that the components of the sounds are clearly distinguishable. Students already know the place of listening in hearing. A listening where there is a presence of the self in one's ears and distractions kept out by one's will. The students have to provide this; without it retention is unlikely. The teacher can only hope it is given and can perhaps urge students to give it, but cannot force it.

It is, therefore, important to relate to the students so that they find it is easy and in their interest to listen. One way of doing it, is to ban repetition. If students know they may not hear that sound again, they may feel they must take their opportunity when it happens. A condition for good hearing is that the sound received is clearly articulated and has enough energy to reach everyone of the students, hence our "loud and clear" rule for the utterance by the voice carrying the new sound to the ears of the students.

But because we do not speak with our ears, we must transfer the information received by the ear to the vocal system that will utter the sound. We must remember that as babies we all constructed a very elaborate system of connections between our voluntary system of sound production and our analytic inner ear and our brain complexes of cells so that we know from the contact of the self at work in our vocal system and indirectly from the impact of these utterances upon our ears what we utter directly. In months of minute surveying and monitoring of the two systems and their connection, we form a unified system, which is capable of analyzing all sounds emitted by outsiders and of using our own voice to produce the equivalent of what we hear. This unified system is demanded by the apprenticeship of learning to speak the language of the environment. Except for the deaf, we all manage to make it as a fine and responsive instrument that serves us well through all of our life. Its having become automatic requires that a special awareness restore the connection between hearing and uttering. Hence our suggestion that we find a way of making students of a new language work first on their voluntary system and hear themselves producing the sounds rather than a model. In this way, every student *knows* directly whether he or she is doing what is required to produce all the component sounds of the new language and *works* at establishing the criteria (somatic and perceptive) which ensure that these sounds are recognizable with the ears and through the brain with the vocal system.

As teachers alerted to the complexity of the task, we have to concentrate upon our own listening of what the students produce, and develop an arsenal of signals that students can understand in order to convey to them what they have to embark on doing in order to produce the required sounds. The relationship with the students is such that it makes it possible for the student to work precisely and solely on what needs to be put right.

Once the students understand the signals, they can use these to tell themselves what to do to put things right. Because in language there is no truth, only agreement with what the natives do, to put things right is to manage to produce deliberately what the natives produce spontaneously. In this the teacher has a place; the students must know they were right at a particular moment, and my rule is that every time I let something pass the students can conclude it is acceptable either as right, or at least is a sufficiently good approximation in the circumstances.

Hence students know that they have either done well, or well enough, or need to work on something to improve their performance.

The teacher must have criteria to let things pass. These criteria sometimes need to be known by the students and sometimes they can be accepted by them as part of the ritual (the mystery) of the student-teacher relationship. No doubt these are real and will soon be part of the functioning of the students, but there is no urgency to make students be concerned with them.

In fact, here we are touching again the dual contrast between teacher and student and student and language.

The teacher has two functions with respect to the students:

- he must force awareness,
- he must provide exercises to insure facility.

To force awareness is to generate situations which are unambiguous and lead inescapably to the recognition that what they hear must be the expression of what they perceive.

To insure facility will mean different things in different circumstances: sometimes it may simply mean that a particularly unfamiliar sound must be uttered again and again until the trend towards its production is clearly visible; sometimes it will mean that a cluster of words are respectively allocated to variations in the situation, sometimes it will mean going over a painstakingly formed sentence with lots of variables until it is uttered with ease and almost spontaneously, and so on.

The students too have two functions, both related to the language. For that reason the teacher should not become a preoccupation of the students.

One is to let the situation have an impact on them as a verbal trigger.

The other one is to integrate the new vocabulary to what was already there by making what was there adequate to meet the new.

Both awareness and facility are realities we can make plain to all as part of the "evaluation" of what is going on, we can consider any recognition as a reality of either an access to awareness or one of the signs of facility. These "objective" signs differ with the area we work on, but their presence can be considered as a universal pointer, marker, or measure, according to which jargon we use.

Awareness is recognized by its attributes just as facility is. But the attributes of awareness can be concomitant with signs of clumsiness and hesitancy that do not appear when we look at an established facility.

It is possible, for instance, to be aware of a sound of the new language and remain unable to produce it for some time: hours, days or even months. Awareness and facility are so different still, no one can say how long facility has lagged behind awareness once the particular sound is being produced correctly.

The signs of awareness without facility may be in the readiness of the students to try again and again to sort out how they have to act on their soma to produce the sounds; to use their intellect to make sense of words uttered by the teacher (such as "Not so far in your throat," or "Keep some saliva in your mouth," or "Don't make it go through your nose," etc.); to watch what *they* are doing. From such awarenesses they will know that to order *their* voluntary vocal system depends on listening to what *they* hear, what *they* are producing, and how to use *their* experience to affect *their* utterances.

Awareness is required in order to proceed in any activity that leads to facility. For the students it is awareness of some functionings, for the teacher it is awareness of that awareness which is needed; otherwise, there is no chance of doing the right things knowingly. Perhaps this point is the cardinal one to keep in mind if we want to say that we actually know what we are doing when teaching. In the case of facility it is obvious that if more words are uttered, more structures are recognized and used in a manner that tells us that the students are getting on top of their difficulties, we have reached an implicit measure which can even be made numerical, if so desired.

How many words can be uttered properly and how long it takes to reach the mastery implied by that? How long can the statements be which can

- be retained after being silently pointed to on the charts?

- be uttered with the proper melody to convey meanings to natives?

- be indicated by the students on the charts?

- be written down without error by the students after visual dictation?

- be read properly from the writing of a colleague who tries his best to be legible?

- be remembered the next lesson or on later occasions?

Facility is measurable because a) it is concerned with time, b) it does refer to lengths of statements, c) it can be related to complexity and d) to the intricacies of the new language as known to natives.

It becomes possible, therefore, to propose a sequence of steps in the classroom which are activities aiming at particular masteries that reflect facility in the various areas. These steps can be associated with "measures" that tell us all the time that teachers are doing the right thing because their students are managing to be on top of the work in every lesson; they too are doing the right thing then.

Thus it is possible (returning to what we spelled out in Chapter 6) to give successively the color names of 9 different rods and note how long it takes students to be able to trigger at once the appropriate names. Soon after, when plurals and the words *one, two,* and *and* are assimilated, the test can become—using a sequence of rods containing one or two of each of the rods being given—how long would it take to obtain:

- a sequence of adequate utterances in response to the sequence pointed at by the teacher, one sequence for each student, and

- a speedy utterance of each of those sequences (speedy, meaning the sounds are uttered as fast as the rods pointed to and as natives would do in the same situation).

For that field we can say that facility has been attained if this is noted. We can make a note of the number of times students have to be asked before they get involved in specific activities that use the words or structures presented. If these requests diminish in number as we advance in the course, this definitely says that the students have recognized in their learning what is effective and have been able to use it more systematically.

When we come to the field of structures, it is clear that awareness here means what most people call understanding. Students will know what some words correspond to and what is generated by the presence of some functional words, such as *not, and, if,* etc., which affect the whole of a statement. Facility will be attained when the students in addition to the order of words required by a structure, manage by themselves to use the new orders; these may correspond to a negative, passive, or a question form *felt* by a student as a response to what is at the source of a statement. Hence we are now confronting two meanings of facility, one strictly within the frame of reference of what has been studied and assimilated, and one beyond that frame of reference expressing the confidence of the students that transformations exist, are known and can be used to generate "variations" on previous themes.

Of course there are meanings of facility which are not included in the above and require a lot more acquaintance with the language than we are considering here. For instance, when we have made it clear what is covered by *give to, give, give back to* and find that the students have no problems with their use, we still have no way of conveying to them the meaning of *give in* or *give up*. The context for these is very different from what makes what we show with the rods possible. Hence there can be no question of including in the measure of facility with the word *give* the whole set of words or expressions derived from it. We can see in what we did in Chapter 7 the bridges to such facilities and only then attempt to assess whether our students have progressed to that level. The various languages taught at present by The Silent Way have challenged us differently. It is our deliberate choice to consider that what we want to give our students first does not cover the social field. Hence our students would show no knowledge at all, in the beginning, of the vocabulary considered by many teachers as the purpose of teaching language: cultural and social intercourse. This kind of facility can be acquired easily at a certain stage, but it does not provide learners with an entry into the language and its spirit, which is our initial purpose.

What we measure as progress is the mastery of all the many changes that result from alterations of situations in time, distance, number, relationship, and the spontaneous utterances that 1) take the essence of a situation into account by triggering some words and not others, some structures and not others and 2) suggest alterations or transformations of either the situation or the corresponding statements when a change is proposed for either. This, of course, covers a huge number of statements and one has to have first reached awareness that there are elements that remain stable in the many possible statements and others that can and do change according to some perceptible alteration in the situation. After that awareness has been secured, the facility is measured by the swiftness and the exactitude of the changes. Once the mastery of the requirement of the verbal changes is obtained, the only thing available is the widening of the field in which new requirements will ask for new awarenesses and new facilities.

Therefore, we can imagine progress taking place in layers of activities which follow each other in time and are concerned with specific demands of the continuous mastery of chunks of the language. These are hierarchically necessary to lead as quickly as possible to as much as possible of the language needed by natives for all their purposes.

In The Silent Way we have selected to concentrate first on the functional vocabulary, although in this book we started even before that when we worked on facility in uttering at the very beginning, and we gave numeration as a field of practice and application of the acquired skills. The functional vocabulary is co-extensive with the grammar of the language and its set of structures. Hence we can measure progress in that layer by the two tools of awareness and facility, provided we exclude even the most common nouns, verbs and adjectives not needed to give students the mastery we are looking for. A verb such as *think* may be excluded within this context; an adjective such as *beautiful* also, and of course most nouns. All these will be needed in another layer.

Going back to Chapter 6 we can find the material that will enter into the evaluation of what has been achieved in the teaching. In most of the languages we have worked on we have about a dozen word charts, of which two or three are to serve as bridges from layer 2 and layer 3 and refer to family relations, the calendar and social time. The rest is strictly used to give the students facility with the structures of the language and its idiosyncrasies. Within layer 1 we expect that progress will be made to the point that almost all students will know how to describe a spatial situation constructed with the rods (to be replaced in layer 2 by many other objects), being sure of how to tackle the situation (this is not obvious at once) and put into one correct statement exactly what they are looking at, as a native would. This implies that the cluster of words for space relations (*near, against each other, standing apart, across, on top, under, above, parallel, on its side, perpendicular to each other, close, far, in the middle, at both ends* (or *one end*), *balancing, symmetrical, skew, forming a tower, forming a wall, above, below, between, to the left, on the right, in front, behind, sideways,* and a few others) is known and triggered by what is presented to the students' sight—though not necessarily all of them by one situation.

There are several clusters of words on the charts, as described in Chapter 6, and the measure of progress at this stage in that layer, is that each of these clusters can be triggered, as it would be for natives and as it would be in one's own language, by a perceptible component in a situation and as a set of substitutes of what one sees.

This layer is by far the most important when we think of making our students free, since in this layer we find the support of the grammar, this is, of what gives us the network of structures that will hold all the special words which reflect the singularity of a given situation. When *rod* is the only noun, students see the form of the statement uttered as belonging to *this* situation and as reflecting its reality. That form then can belong to the next layers as well. Indeed, when new objects are introduced what will be shifted from such statements to the needed ones will be recognized as more pervasive and as referring to the form of the statements rather than to the words. This feeling is the one we associate with structures of the language and with grammar. If the awareness has been reached and the students acknowledge their facility with the functional language as it applies to rods, we can say that they have learned the grammar of the language, even if subtleties that result from special concepts and fine shades of meaning evoked by certain words in certain circumstances (as in the case of irony) are missed. In this layer the accumulation of the masteries of the clusters will form the basis for the measure of progress. We can, during our lessons, see that the students are indeed on top of every one of these demands, which end up in a spontaneous triggering of the "correct" structures including the "correct words" and also see them move on to the next set of masteries.

No special occasion for a particular test is needed in the field of languages if we want to know that our students have done their share of the work towards mastery, precisely because 1) the functional vocabulary does not need to be remembered and is truly retained as proved by its recurrent usage, 2) we have been careful not to move ahead until ogdens were paid, and until the clusters have become functional with the practice. Still if a test is given at any time, the students would take it in their stride having reached the capacity to work like natives at that level.

We have indicated in the previous chapters how we can generate awareness of shades of meanings, and we understand that this has to be done not only in one area but in every one of those covered by the functional vocabulary; therefore, what we mentioned above for space relations will also have taken place for temporal relations (*after, before, while, at the same time, during, immediately, soon after, earlier, later, when, whenever, in between, simultaneously, for a while, then, since, slowly, swiftly, quickly, rhythmically,* etc.) for causation (*because, since, what, by the way, necessarily, probably, likely, surely, certainly, no doubt, in vain, inevitably, still, yet,* etc.) for quantification (*a few, some, several, many, all, much, less, more, increase, decrease, handful, lots, a lot, including, inclusive, part of* etc); for inclusion and exclusion (*belongs, part of, within, without, out of, in, left over, take away, remove, add, widen, broaden, separate, unite, together, in a set, one by one, two by two,* etc.); for generalization * (*those who, those which, all, all but, most, the majority, every, everybody, everyone, everywhere, no one, none, nobody, seldom, often, by the way, occasionally, rarely, once upon a time, frequently, from time to time, sporadically, regularly, on call,* etc.) and so on.

---

* Pronouns could be included in this list since they replace classes of nouns, but we do not write them in here.

In Chapter 9 we worked on layers 2 and 3 and most of Chapter 7 is concerned with layer 4 because of the stress on colloquialisms and sayings in the new language. There is, of course, a layer 5 about which we shall write in the next and last chapter of this book.

What we proposed in Chapter 9 for the expansion of vocabulary did not necessarily involve the systematic expansion of the uses of the functional vocabulary on the charts that was taken up in Chapter 7. It is possible to progress in the use of the language by making the functional vocabulary available for the study of the pictures and the vocabulary of "A Thousand Sentences."

To measure progress in these areas we have first the tool of the worksheets. Indeed we have seen how the students' productions can serve as documents to ascertain that the students have a) acquired several hundred words (mainly nouns, adverbs, and adjectives); b) acquired the facility of including them in their own sentences, observing the grammar of the language, its spellings, the meanings they want to convey; c) acquired the confidence and the facility to produce their spontaneous compositions on themes of their own choosing based on the impact of a picture.

When we look at the worksheets, we can associate numerical scores to what is done in page 1, on page 2, on page 3 and even if it is harder, on page 4. These figures could serve, if need be, as a measure of progress in this layer and indicate that so and so has indeed reached a mastery of what is being studied, or is a certain distance from it. The latter can provide the teacher with the information concerning the kind and amount of practice that is needed by the students in question to reach the mastery required (i.e., comparable to what the average native is known to be able to do in the study of that language in a community having it as its own language).

There is no doubt that the worksheets provide data in the four areas of acquiring certain vocabularies; giving evidence of treating that vocabulary like natives do, as triggers of one or more meanings; knowing how to involve new words and the functional vocabulary in correct statements within certain conditions; knowing how to use all one has to produce a piece of writing entirely on one's own which is loosely linked to a set of conditions.

If the last test is "quantified" by counting the words used in the composition, the number of words per sentence, the number of correct spellings, the number of correct structures, the number of non-functional words used, the number of colloquialisms used, we shall have an assessment of progress in the realm of facility with each of the underlying components. But there is more to this test; for instance, the personal qualities that come through the writing such as sense of humor, daring, imagination, aptness of images, precision and conciseness, all of which are not easily associated with scores but are accessible to a teacher and certainly can serve to indicate how students link to the new language, and thus give a measure of progress.

This could already have been applied to what appears on page 3 of the worksheets. But when we come to the progress to be accomplished with the content of the book "A Thousand Sentences," we need to develop new tools.

In Chapter 8 we mentioned translation as an instrument to which we can resort when we want to know whether students have got a meaning from an exercise in which words alone have been used. This could be used here, too, but it may serve no purpose as a measure to a teacher who may not be able to connect with the language or languages of his or her students. So translation has a very restricted part to play in the evaluation although it is perfectly adequate as a precise measure of the understanding of the content of a book.

If the relationship of a teacher to his or her class is such that trust exists, and the understanding of the seriousness of the contribution of each one to the work of the other has served to move ahead, it may be possible that a nod on the part of the students to the question, "Did you get the meaning of this sentence" is sufficient to allow the class to move on. Since rods can be counted as well as the number of the sentences read, their number may serve as a "measure" in this layer.

For those who cannot accept this as a measure, we need to provide a different approach. We already know that each sentence can be read aloud, and we can give tally to the number of phrasings missed, the presence or absence of intonation and melody. These figures refer to the act of reading, which may reach a level we may call "perfection," when it is as good as that of good native's reading.

As to comprehension, we can sometimes find that the production of a drawing or a cutting from a publication or a construction with the rods may imply it; or sometimes a paraphrase or a definition, an equivalent expression is all that is needed. For example, sentences 55, 63 in "A Thousand Sentences" can be illustrated with cuttings or pictures; sentences 40 and 205 are definitions; sentence 495 cannot be illustrated since it expresses an opinion, but can be understood if one's experience suggests it is true; sentence 735 is a definition but implies so much that we cannot say that the definition conveys its own meaning as it is generally expected. Here we need a great deal more to be sure that we comprehend, and translation may be the most economical route.

To assess the progress of comprehension of a written text which does not refer to an action that can be carried out; nor to things that can be brought about actually or via reproduction in print; nor to notions that can be shown in a diagram, a classification or a table, but to summaries of experiences and inner life components, we have to accept to wait till the students themselves use spontaneously the words, phrases and sayings, and do make sense for us. We can then conclude that they have reached the level of facility in their layer. If we need more permanent evidence, we can collect from the work of our students the statements they make and classify them for what facility they demonstrate. This, of course, will be the case for layer 4 when what we did in Chapter 7 has to be assessed for impact. But it is also present in layer 3.

A test we would *not* use would be one in which we give *a priori* a set of words and enquire whether students know how to use them. Such a test would involve our judgment of what needs to be known of the language rather than what the students have done so far. It would tell as much what students do not know, or rather what they are not prepared to bring forth, as what they do know. To "measure" progress is much more to determine what students have actually done, not how far they are from where a cultured native is.

In all our work we have been guided by what we call common sense. If we want to know what a student knows, what is the value of finding much of what he or she does *not* know? In the case of a certain whole that can be divided into two complementary parts, the finding of one would be equivalent to the finding of the other. But since languages are not such wholes, and since knowledge can mean many things, we need to develop the sensitivities that will bring us to the point where we can say that certain awarenesses needed to progress in one's study of a language are available and that, related to such awarenesses, facilities have reached such levels mainly so that we can suggest exercises that lead to greater facilities approximating those of natives. The term "natives" is to be represented in the classroom by the teacher, not by the most talented writer of the language. Teachers' own achievements set the standard of what we are to achieve with our pupils. If pupils can be as good as their teacher, we must express our contentment.

In the beginning of this book we referred several times to this criterion and found that it was a reasonable measure of what we would aim at in the fields of pronunciation, of flow of words, of numeration and arithmetic. The same criterion is valid throughout because we are concerned with classroom teaching in schools and because language teachers are recruited from among those who apply for posts and they are what they are, not necessarily the most competent linguists or writers in the community.

To "measure" progress in an absolute manner is beyond us and we should not attempt it. We have attempted instead to measure the kind of progress that is possible from the actual duration of the effort to learn the language, from the kind of teacher available, the instruments used and the student population concerned, and this has led us to see in everything that happens in the classroom, when it happens, the evidence of the learning that is to be taken into account if we want to be fair to our students. By using the continuous feedback of what goes on in the classroom not only do we know what we are doing (we represents here students and teachers) but we also find out what needs to be done to increase the yield, i.e., to make progress. Our silence (as teachers) at least ensures the objectivity of the evidence, which can only come from the students. Every exercise we suggested in the previous chapters reaffirms the principle that only what is done by the students can count in our assessment of what we propose in our lessons. Hence we must have evidence at our disposal to justify how we got to the point where we now are. It is this evidence that we want to bring to the tester, particularly if we are ourselves the tester. The problem of evaluation then becomes one of adding a systematic approach to that evidence and this is what we have attempted to cover in this chapter up to the 5th layer, which will be considered in the next chapter.

We know that we can equip each Silent Way teacher with the means to assess progress all the time because the same techniques that are used in the teaching produce the evidence of the learning. Teachers only need to become conscious of this to find ways of not losing the evidence, and even of wanting to understand it better and to gather it for special study. Once available it can be presented as documentation of what happened in the classroom. It would also eliminate a gap in all testing caused by the fact that it is administered on one or two occasions and is unable to cover all the ground while what we recommend does.

In conclusion we need only add that The Silent Way is the best test that has ever been developed because it assesses all the time—and therefore in a fair manner—what students have actually produced for themselves, by themselves, and within the time spent in contact with the challenges of a new language and with their teacher. The material and the techniques teach and test at the same time, with the result that students can learn meaningfully without being mystified or intimidated.

Teachers only need to glean the evidence, study it and classify it for it to become a public assessment of what has gone on in language classes in schools.

11 Short Passages and Stories

As teachers we only have responsibility for our students so long as they are in our classes. For our students the responsibility is continuous and permanent and does not stop at the points where we leave them. They may have all sorts of intentions, dreams, and purposes and may wish to go much further than their teachers and the set curricula go.

Therefore, we shall give ourselves, in a common sense manner, an end to our responsibility as teachers and call it "the final opening," final to us but not to our students.

In The Silent Way we consider our job done when we bring our independent, autonomous and responsible students over the threshold of literature, leaving the whole field open to them, but not taking with them the steps in it. To free our students from the final restrictions before they feel, as natives do, entitled to pick up any book and to relate to the written word in the way they do in their own language, we have had to add two books to "A Thousand Sentences."

In that book students faced sentences one by one, and the writer tried to ease the way into a book by using as often as possible the device of definition. Now the writer wants to be free to handle each subject on its own merits and refuses to be restricted in vocabulary and form. But one more variable can be considered to indicate that the contact with the learners has not been lost, that is, the amount of written material to present the students with. The text consists of more than a few sentences but yet not forcing on learners a huge burden. So "Short Passages" is our solution, and it is not a larger book than "A Thousand Sentences." It offers thirty-six "slices" of life that have been specially written for students of The Silent Way, and it has a special function in the whole scheme. The second volume is made up of "Eight Tales," which although not specially written for The Silent Way have found their place naturally in it as the last step before opening all libraries to our students. We shall treat these two books separately and give more attention to the first because the second is in fact literature and represents the other side of the threshold while the work done on the first will pay handsomely.

Short Passages

Their length varies from 200 to 900 words. The themes covered include a large variety, from four stories about children and teenagers to one about a hermit on a glacier. Included are: social themes, such as welfare, travel, commerce; social events such as concerts, shopping, visits to the doctor, a new dress, buying stamps; natural calamities such as storms, isolated communities, death by drowning; strange occurrences such as fish evading an angler, an angry customer, a shy person, two friends without a common language, an unexpected inheritance; more common events, resting by a fire, learning not to butt in, a scene at the barber shop, looking for a job, enjoying speed on highways, a bridgeplayer team; special concerns such as collecting rare books, wanting a meal in Paris, not being fooled by a friend, occupying oneself while waiting at a doctor's office, and a few more not easily classifiable.

It is a book students can adopt as a reader and use at home.

It is a book which could be adopted by a class and read in class and worked on in various ways as we shall see soon.

Because there are no vocabulary restrictions, it is not artificial in any way. The stories are almost all about events that actually happened but are treated as stories to reach the readers and make an impact. They are intended to touch readers, to make them think, to make them want to talk, to ask questions, to comment, to relate to the subject, to feel that there may be something to learn from them besides vocabularies, punctuation, and the form of sentences. For instance, they can offer students ideas about how to write short stories, how to enter into a subject, how to end a story or leave it without an end, how to use words to produce images, how to tease a reader through some suggestion or provoke him with some incredible proposal, how to blend ideas, images and sounds through a selection of words or the length of sentences. Each piece will have something different to offer because it was the deliberate intention of the writer to move the readers to be concerned with affectivity as well as the intellect. The impressionistic technique of dots placed side by side to generate an impact is used constantly and produces the desired effects.

The vignettes in this book are ends in themselves; they aim at justifying the time students will give to them by the various gains readers will recognize. Teachers may find assistance in these stories, first because they exist, second because they are manageable in one lesson, and third because they will not in general leave students indifferent. The breadth of the topics covered will also help: they may contain something for every taste and every age. The various uses which have been made of them here and there until now tend to confirm this response.

We do not look at these texts as opportunities to make students into literary critics in the sense in which classical texts studied at school tend to do. Their job is to provide:

- continuous reading, which is manageable even if several words are not part of one's vocabulary and need to be looked up in a one-language dictionary or in a two-language one;

- means to decide whether a statement in the new language when read does affect one's mind in the way reading in one's language does, i.e., generates images, feelings, and thoughts that one can consider in contrast with the rest of one's experience;

- examples of sentences that meet some demands beyond the vocabulary, spelling, grammar, or even literary reference, such as style, sophistication of expression, capacity to affect, contribution to the creation of a specific climate;

- examples of descriptions, of discussions, of presentations of a view, of argumentation, of attempts at inspiration, of attempts at touching, or mobilizing at circumscribing an issue, at characterization of persons or situations;

- examples of how to engage readers, of the role of the first sentence and of how to charge readers so that they remain thoughtful;

- and finally they provide an opportunity to see how much has not been done that may invite readers to supply themselves in their uniqueness and the uniqueness of their lives.

There may not be much time in a second language course to be thorough in all these studies. Each teacher will confront particular situations in himself/herself and his or her classes and will select to enter one or other of the suggested activities or invent new ones. What we can do here is to work on one example to open up avenues that can lead to a pinpointed evaluation of what students do at this level.

Mark and Teresa

In their class were a few boys and girls who were much more interested in each other than in what the teacher had to offer. Mark and Teresa were two who believed they had fallen in love.

Teresa was slim and pretty: Mark would try to look elegant, paying a great deal of attention to his appearance. He went to the hairdresser every week, bought shirts and trousers and would change his style often while most of his friends were content to wear the same outfit for some time.

Teresa wanted Mark to look after her and for ever to be her squire. Mark accepted this when it satisfied his vanity, but would sulk and refuse to do what Teresa asked if he thought it would lower his self-esteem. At first glance, it seemed that these two young people, engaged in getting the best out of life, would find it easy to get on together. But life has its own ways of testing every one of us, however clever or happy we are. Teresa believed firmly that her good looks gave her some right over anyone who happened to admire her. Mark had yielded for a time, and this strengthened her belief until she came to expect everyone to accept her view of life unquestioningly. So she became very unhappy when quite naturally Mark once smiled back at a girl in the class who had begun to find him attractive.

Teresa was present in the lesson, but her mind was elsewhere. Pat's and Mark's exchange of smiles, surely part of the daily currency of the class, became for Teresa the most tormenting event. She felt betrayed, all her love and all her life in danger, and had to use all her self-control to hold back the tears and the cry of pain that accompanied her discovery of such meanness in the knight who had given her his promise.

Mark felt the terrific tension mounting in his neighbor. He knew the cause since, although his smile to Pat had contained an understanding of her interest in him, he would not admit this to Teresa. Their *sotto voce* conversation went on all through the lesson. Completely absorbed in her feelings of grief, Teresa saw her world reduced to Mark, Pat and herself, though her self-control prevented the teacher from noticing anything unusual. Mark tried to be self-righteous in his replies, refusing to consider himself a traitor—which was all Teresa wanted from him. He could have regained her confidence had he promised not to smile at Pat again, Pat who suddenly became a rival to Teresa. Instead, he denied her the knowledge of what was going on inside him when he smiled. It hurt her most that the boy she liked best was refusing her the intelligence of the things of the heart, denying her sense of truth at work.

The lesson over, Teresa dragged Mark outside by the hand to the most isolated bench in the playground. Violently she poured out her grief, but succeeded only in bringing out the worst in him. His answers were sharp and unkind. His sympathy diminished every minute. Teresa hardly found it possible to go to the staff room and ask to be excused for the rest of the day.

At home she shut herself up in her room crying and swearing to give up Mark, yet crying for her love and wishing to forgive him if only...

Meanwhile Mark started courting Pat who at this moment seemed so much more attractive than Teresa.

There are in this short text a number of elements that can serve the students in relating to the language for what it can do to increase one's grasp of reality. Printed words lose a little of their fleetingness because the ink sinks into the paper, but they only become alive because we link with them, sound them, entertain them. Still words are only triggers and they trigger mental states which are impermanent, can replace each other, push each other out of consciousness and generate collectively a mood that can be more lasting, more lingering than any impression or image.

This can be "measured" simply by looking at a clock or watch and finding out how long particular students maintain their interest in what is brought to them by the vignette.

If there is a response from the students, a number of literary questions may arise that can be related to a study of the text to find evidence for what one thinks.

For example, is a reader made to think of himself or herself rather than the trio in the story? Does a reader start by saying: "It reminds me of . . . " "I know what . . . feels: I went through it myself on one (or more) occasion . . . " This is objective evidence for what reading a text does to readers.

If instead someone says: "While I can picture Mark and Teresa, I do not find anything to pin down an image about Pat," it is clear that the reader has remained with the text and has analyzed it to the point of knowing something definite about it. He could be asked by the teacher: "Do you think it was done deliberately by the author?" or "Do you think the author, by withholding information about Pat, is forcing us to remain with something else he has in mind?" In such a way the student or the class finds another reason to work more deeply on the material.

Finding evidence in a text for what emerges in one's mind is what will help students to become more critical and more appreciative of literary productions.

Questions that may stimulate research of that evidence will be sought by teachers. A few examples for this text could be:

- Does the writer let facts speak for themselves or does he butt in to interfere with the reader and share his beliefs or experience when he could have chosen not to? What about lines 17 and 18?

- How much do we know about Mark? about Teresa? Are they given equally as much build-up? Who is a more complex character? Do you have impressions of them you can put in words? Do you have impressions about them that present themselves in your mind as you evoke each of them?

- Which statements strike you as carriers of qualities that contribute to the creation of

    1   special climate for the story of for certain moments in it?

    2   a particularly apt insight in yourself, in others, in the workings of the mind, or of passion, or of self-centeredness?

    3   images that can be called vivid, dull, fuzzy, complex, presenting some relief?

     4   data about the situation or the characters?

- Can you answer the following questions and find the evidence for the truth of your answers?

     1   how old are the heroes of the story?

     2   what is their social position?

     3   what was the way they were taught in their lessons?

     4   what sort of school were they in?

- Are there only issues about love relations in the circumstances of these characters? or can we detect other issues? where is the evidence?

- Can you detect in this short passage ways of working of the writer that produce feelings that you might qualify as aesthetic, as of any significance for you, as capable of widening your awareness of who you are and how you relate? Can you give the elements of the text which cause the various feelings?

- After how many sentences did you become interested in the story? Is there a special role given to the first sentence in the writer's mind? Is this true of first sentences in the other passages in this book? Is it the case for all short stories? Can authors afford to discourage readers at the beginning, or is it common sense that the threshold to a story should have the quality of holding whoever looks at it?

- Can you find what qualifications may make final sentences into good ones as far as leaving the reader with a definite impact from a writing? Begin with the one in this passage and then look at other passages in this book and, whenever possible, look at ends of short stories.

- Look again at the various paragraphs in this passage. Can you see why the author separated them one from the other? Do you feel that they balance each other? Get as much evidence from the paragraphs to criticize or justify the use of paragraphing as a means of helping readers come more easily to the author's aims.

- Can you think of an author as someone who takes responsibility for what he confides to us on paper? as doing things deliberately, i.e., choosing what needs saying and what can be left out? choosing the length of the story, the paragraphs, the sentences and the words he uses because of their sonority, capacity to trigger images, feelings, thoughts? In particular using artifacts to keep readers interested, to involve them affectively, intellectually, socially, to increase some impacts and reduce others? If you do, you have valid criteria to relate through a text to a writer; that is if you want to!

There may be other questions that would come to teachers engaged in providing literary education in a new language. For instance, whether translation of these passages would help the expanded awareness of the language and would come closer to what a passage has to offer and then suggest translations.

Teachers may want to handle vocabularies that do not refer to objects or are functional in areas of experience studied by human scientists, and also vocabularies that are concerned with aesthetic awareness, with reflection and personal mental growth. In this book there are a number of passages that are opportunities for such growth beyond the literary and the literal.

Taking examples of the kind of "slices" of life represented in this book, teachers may encourage their students to look for opportunities to capture the singular in the familiar and the current and to expand with other students' works the net of what is worth preserving.

"Short Passages" is not a collection of short stories. For this we turn to a book of "Eight Tales" which is offered as a further contribution to students' literary education in the new language.

Whether this book is adopted or not, students will want to know whether they have advanced enough in the language to remain in contact with the sinews of a larger writing and its demands. But because a short story offers a different frame of reference from that offered by a short passage concerned with almost anything, a contact with short stories will make students aware that they can live through a lot more and perhaps be as inspired and rewarded for the effort of remaining for that long with a demanding passage than with short passages.

The "Eight Tales" were written for readers of any age and have a number of functions in education. They present cultural opportunities through the four oriental tales. They include symbolic treatments of life themes disguised in the contents of stories. They give occasion for some free rein of the imagination and of devices that story tellers indulge in. They cover a space-time stretch so indefinite that they transcend cultures and civilizations although the appearances stress these. They invite one to dream and to think and they add to one's life what can be done in the virtual realm. They aim at bringing the reader back to himself, even though they take the route of strange experiences.

More profound literary questions can be asked simply because there are more opportunities in a longer text. For instance, how does a writer hold a reader's interest for so long? What artifacts are being used to move the story along and keep it going? How can one decide whether enough has been said? Could more have been said? Which are the criteria used by the writer to sense that what is done is worth doing and in the way it has been done?

Because these three books are part of The Silent Way materials, it is possible to study the latitude given a writer with more space to do what he may want to do; for the reader, about the topics, for the writer's realization of his idea of a literary work that may aim at being a work of art, a work of love!

Abandoning more and more restrictions clearly serves readers and writers. The flexibility of writing within flexible conditions is experienced immediately by anyone examining the three books, and this can be extrapolated from short stories to novels of any size. While opportunities occur with every expansion, demands grow at the same time and writers must find resources in themselves not asked of them earlier. Students of literature can experience the opportunities and the demands, both of which are part of their education as writers and as sensitive readers.

In the original proposal for The Silent Way, the final opening into the literature of the new language included a set of three anthologies. Fifteen years later the project has not yet become a publisher's reality although the preliminary work has been done in three languages. We shall not consider here their function as we see it in the literary education of foreign language students. Those interested in this question can read in Chapter 4 of "Teaching Foreign Languages in Schools" what we had to say originally and which remains our view of the matter in its broad terms.

We have been guided in our final opening and in all the preceding chapters through what seems to us to be common sense. It is common sense because it comes naturally to anyone who remains in contact with the challenge. For us the mere fact that we work with people and let them take it as their responsibility to reach constantly a sense of naturalness with the new language dictates our avoiding bright ideas and concentrating instead on pinpointed tasks that free students in a precise manner, more and more. Language is no more vocabularies to be memorized than structures to be practiced or expressions to be assimilated. It is a functioning of man as wide as all he experiences and can express. Besides words, there is the wealth of inner dynamics that accompany them, precedes them in the case of the writers and follows them in the case of readers. The opening into literature is to give students the certainty that all that man can express in his native language is also expressible in the new one, if the literature has already done it. If not, it will be part of the evolution of that language to involve itself in the innovations required.

Appendices

French

Tableaux 1

Exemples du type A.

Deux à deux. La brune est là. Il est rouge. Elle? ici? Elle ici! A elles deux. Oui et non. Vous deux. Non! non! non! Oui oui! A nous deux. A eux deux. Lui aussi? Et moi? Ici aussi. A moi!

Exemples du type B.

A la une. Prenez-moi. Nez à nez. Elle est jaune. J'ai votre oui. A boire! Bougez-vous! Donnez-lui la note. J'ai les bleus. Elle vote aussi. Donnez-vous à lui. La lune est jaune. Ici et là.

Exemples du type C.

- Nous avons ici des noirs, des jaunes et des rouges.
- Elles ont les verts, moi j'ai les bleus.
- Elle, lui et moi, nous nous mettons ici, et vous, vous vous mettez là.
- Lui, il est là, elle, non.
- Vous, vous êtes aussi rouge?

Tableaux 1 et 2

Exemples du type A

Qui n'en a pas? Qu'est-ce que c'est? Ils n'en sont pas. Que c'est bien! N'est-ce pas? Comment! elle aussi? Bonjour vous deux! Qui m'appelle? De jour en jour. Aussi bien l'une que l'autre. Ce n'est pas à lui. Quel son! Quel jour avons-nous?

Exemples du type B

Comme vous le prenez! Quel appel! Pas un des leurs n'est là. Comment ne pas l'appeler! Eh oui! Ils en sont là. Elle en a vu des vertes. Elle en est rouge. Ne le prenez pas comme ca! N'y mettez pas le nez. Bien le bonjour. Bien à vous. Ne vous en prenez qu'à vous.

Exemples du type C

- Les miens vont bien, comment vont les vôtres?
- Les couleurs sont si belles que je ne me m'en lasse pas.
- Les amis de vos amis sont mes amis.
- Remettez-le lui en mon nom, sinon elle ne le prendra pas.
- Mettez au clair ce que vous avez à dire.
- Je sais quels sont mes droits et mes devoirs, vous n'avez pas à me les dire.

Tableaux 1, 2 et 3

Exemples du type A

D'avant en arrière. Mettez-vous à 1'arrière. Où en est-il? Quelle surprise! Qui n'en est pas surpris? Il l'a prise par surprise. Je suis pris. Elle est très prise. Violà ce que c'est! Voilà où j'en suis. De plus en plus. Qui suis-je? Suis-moi. Et comment! Allons, allons! Çà et là.

Exemples du type B

Il en est épris. De votre suite, j'en suis. Qu'en est-il de lui? Arrière de moi, satan! Elle l'a remis à l'endroit. C'est mon droit. A qui de droit. Qu'il est gauche. Il est pris de court. Il lui court après. Prenez le surplus. Rien ne va plus. A chacun son dû. Mettez-y du vôtre. A même le sol. Sens dessus dessous.

Exemples du type C

- Mettez-les de côtè, ce n'est pas pour moi.
- Petits et grands vont au-devant de lui.
- Plus il en a, moins il en donne.
- Donnez-moi vos sous, vous en avez plus que moi.
- Comment savez-vous que ses dessous sont blancs?
- Par dessus tout, cela m'a plu, à vous aussi?
- Qui plus est, elle est à moi.
- De quel droit l'avez-vous pris, ce n'est pas très adroit.
- D'après lui, c'est elle qui le lui a donné.
- Etes-vous à raême de le suivre?
- Lui, il est très à gauche et elle, elle est encore plus à gauche.
- Il marche derrière elle, il la suit, il l'appelle, il l'appelle encore, et elle, elle fait mine de rien, elle continue son chemin.

Tableaux 1-4

Exemples du type A

Seul à seul. Loin de là. De loin en loin. On en est encore loin. S'il vous plaît. Plaît-il? Assez! Je vous en remercie. Merci bien. Pas de quoi. Pas un seul! Encore! D'homme à homme. Entre femmes.

Exemples du type B

Elle revient de loin! Maintenant, on y revient. Tenez-vous bien! J'y tiens . . . je suis à votre merci. Ne lui tombez pas dessus. Tenez-le en laisse. N'en jetez plus. Tenez-vous en là. Il se tient coi. Un homme à la mer! Est-ce encore loin? J'en ai plus qu'assez. Sa famme l'a laissé tomber.

Exemples du type C

- Le petit est tombé sur son derrière.
- L'un dans l'autre, ça revient au même.
- Laissez-le seul avec elle maintenant, s'il vous plaît.
- Regardez ces hommes et ces femmes, ne sont-ils pas encore jeunes?
- Il est venu ici seul, et voilà que maintenant sa fille vient aussi.
- Donnez m'en un petit peu plus, ça me plaît.
- La plus grande des petites filles est plus grande

que le plus petit des grands garçons. -

- Ouvrez la boîte et regardez donc ce qu'il y a dedans.

Tableaux 1-5

Exemples du type A

Elle s'y est mise. Quel ensemble! Dans l'ensemble, ça va bien. Qu'y pouvons-nous? Peu à peu. Je n'en peux plus. Je ne lui en veux pas. C'est à prendre ou à laisser. Elle a mis son ensemble rouge. Vous y pouvez beaucoup. Quelles sommes! Entrez, entrez!

Exemples du type B

Ça vous prend au ventre. Il est un peu m'as-tu-vu. Il va en mettre un coup. Quel mets, et quels entremets! Il est entré dans le jeu. A vos jeux. Les dés sont jetés. Il est dans le coup. C'est du beau! C'en est trop. C'est bien peu. Il est bien mis. Quel va-et-vient.

Exemples du type C

- Dites-vous bien que je n'en ai pas la moindre idée.
- Nous nous sommes mis à deux pour l'attraper.
- Quand nous sommes entre nous, nous pouvons nous laisser aller.
- Regardez-y d'un petit peu plus près.
- Il m'a dit qu'il y a mis beaucoup du sien.
- Sortez de là, parce que s'il vous y prend, il va se mettre à vous battre.

- Laissez-le ici encore quelques mois, ça lui fait du bien.

- Vous pouvez encore nous rattraper, parce que les jeux ne sont pas encore faits.

Tableaux 1-6

Exemples du type A

Du tout au tout. Tout à fait. Tout au plus. Tout au moins. A qui mieux mieux. Surtout pas. Rien du tout. C'est un fait. Nom de nom! Vous n'y êtes pour rien. A une seconde près. C'est vite fait.

Exemples du type B

Je suis refait. Ce n'est pas le tout. Il a tout pour plaire. Un pour tous, tous pour un. Il lui a foncé dessus. A la tombée du jour. Elle le seconde bien. Il n'est pas très bien secondé. Ça ne me fait rien.

Exemples du type C

- C'est bien fait, vous n'aviez qu'à ne pas le laisser sortir.

- Vous n'y êtes pas du tout, au nom de quoi faites-vous cela?

- A quoi bon, ne vous en faites pas, cela ne sert de rien.

- Puisque la plupart d'entre eux sont ici, pourquoi ne pas les laisser jouer ensemble?

- A eux tous, ils en font moins que lui tout seul.
- Puisque vous ne le faites pas, qu'est-ce que vous en savez?

Tableaux 1-7

Exemples du type A

Deux c'est assez, trois c'est trop. C'en est trop. Merci mille fois. Il est à moitié fou. C'est la moitié moins. A demi mot. C'est moins une. Revenez demain en huit. Cent pour cent. Elle monte les marches quatre à quatre.

Exemples du type B

En cinq sept. En quatrième vitesse. Faites-le devant un tiers. Le tiers et le quart. De sept en quatorze. Il fait les quatre cents coups. Je vous le donne en mille. A malin, malin et demi. C'est quatre fois pire. Vous avez tapé dans le mille. Le tiers monde. Elle se met en quatre pour lui.

Exemples du type C

- Est-ce que vous prenez un demi de rouge avec moi?
- Trois petits tours et puis s'en vont.
- N'allez pas chez lui aujourd'hui, car de dix à midi il sera sorti.

- Si vous le voulez bien, venez chez moi entre six et huit.

- Qu'est-ce que vous avez à chercher comme ça de midi à quatorze heures?

- Elle est toute seule, qu'a-t-elle fait de sa moitié?

Tableaux 1-8

Exemples du type A

Mais oui! Quoi de neuf! A table! Ça n'en finit plus. Quoi de plus facile? Presque rien. A quoi bon! A point. Par-ci par-là. Parfois c'est impossible. Ni plus ni moins. Quelque peu. En tous points. Quoi qu'il en soit. Quel son!

Exemples du type B

Ça alors! Quelle femme légère! Faites le point. Elle est mal en point. Ne tablez pas trop là-dessus. Ce n'est guère mieux. Ceci n'est pas encore au point. Un bon point pour lui. Il fait du porte à porte. Ce n'est guère mieux.

Exemples du type C

- Il n'y a que le premier pas qui coûte.

- L'homme est un être fini.

- A chaque coup, elle se fait mettre en boîte.

- Il a fini par se mettre à table.

- Est-elle lourde à ce point? —qui l'eut cru?

- Ce sont amis que vent emporte, et il ventait devant ma porte.

- Personne ne se lève aussi facilement que lui.

- Quelquefois elle se met à ses côtés, mais le plus souvent elle s'en va du sien.

Tableaux 1-9

Exemples du type A

Allez-vous en. De temps en temps. Faites le plein. En plein milieu. Jamais plus. Je ne tiens plus debout. Par la suite. Elle est bien mise. A tout jamais. A la prochaine. Tel quel. Par tous les temps. Allez jusqu'au bout. Le train est plein.

Exemples du type B

Quel entrain! Elle n'y tient plus. Il fait des vers. Il fait le vide autour de lui. Le temps d'un éclair. Nous sommes à bout. C'est tout de travers. Quelle poursuite! Les tenants et les aboutissants. Elle lui en fait voir. Mettez-le sur l'autel.

Exemples du type C

- En étant si brutal avec elle, il l'a mise à l'envers.

- Si vraiment vous dites que cela ne va pas, je ferai mieux la prochaine fois.
- Allez-voir un tel de ma part, et faites-lui part de la suite.
- Il y a des vers dedans, il est si vieux.
- Elle s'est mise en plein devant, il n'y a plus moyen de rien voir.
- En nous quittant si tôt, il laisse un grand vide derrière lui.
- C'est inutile de vouloir en reprendre, entretemps il n'en reste plus, il a tout fini.
- Après la pluie le beau temps.

Tableaux 1-10

Exemples du type A

A tort et à travers. Sans rime ni raison. A chacun son dû. Chacun son tour. Vous avez tout à fait raison. C'est un monde! Disons ce qui est. Ainsi soit-il. Tout un chacun. Peu s'en faut. Bord à bord. Justement pas. C'est un peu fort.

Exemples du type B

Bon été. Ça fait pendant. Cela ne me dit rien de bon. Faites-vous une raison. Toujours les mêmes! Au premier abord. Il est d'un abord difficile. Montez à bord. Il est d'un tout autre bord. Il est tordu. Ça lui pend au nez. C'est trop fort.

Exemples du type C

- Un tiens vaut mieux que deux tu l'auras.
- Ne mettez pas vos affaires là, sinon vous aurez affaire à moi.
- Pendant des jours et des jours, sa maison resta sans toît.
- Il était temps, en peu plus et il allait se faire mettre en prison.
- Cela fait longtemps que nous ne prenons que l'avion.
- Ce n'est pas la peine que vous alliez chez lui puisqu'il est ici.
- A vous pour toujours, quoi que vous disiez et quoi que vous fassiez.

Tableaux 1-11

Exemples du type A

La main dans la main. Quelle question! Au vu et au su de tous. Mot à mot. Pas un mot. C'est exact. De haut en bas. Un parmi tant d'autres. Mettez-les en tas. Entre quatre yeux. Pas question! Allez vous reposer. Mettez vos bas noirs. Elle a réponse à tout.

Exemples du type B

Elle tient tout en mains. Rendez la main. Une main de fer. C'est pire que tout. Sois belle et tais-toi. Fermez les yeux là-dessus. Ne vous enfermez pas. C'est du délire. Des mets fins. Le fin du fin. Le jour va poindre. Ces pieux étaient la paroi. Essayez de me joindre demain.

Exemples du type C

- Fermez les yeux, j'ai une surprise pour vous.
- Il ne sera pas dit que nous n'aurons pas eu le dernier mot.
- S'il vous regarde de haut, faites-lui un coup bas.
- Pendant que nous y sommes, voyons au fait qui a raison.
- Parmi tous ceux qui sont ici, combien y en a-t-il qui l'ignore?
- Lorsque tout le monde saura où vous êtes allé, qu'allez-vous pouvoir leur dire?

Italian

Tabella 1

Frasi di tipo A

Non ci vede? Un arancio rosso. Rose rosse e gialle. Sono soli soli. Li prende due a due. Gli dia questo o quello. Mi tagli una mela. Lo nego. Prenda l'uno e l'altro. Pende que e lí. Da lí non ci vede. Non è una tenda. Li appenda qui. Lui mima lei e lei mima me. Vende mele e arance.

Frasi di tipo B

È in bianco e nero. Non c'è altro. Anche lei è verde. È un giallo. Qui non c'è verde. Le prende da lui e da lei. Sono in blu. I Bianchi e i Neri. Ci mette un'ora. Non se la prenda. Lo riprende. Sono nera (nero, neri). La smetta. Mi prenda! Lo dia a quel rosso. Mi arrendo, mi arrendo! Quel giallo tende al verde. Ha messo le tende.

Frasi di tipo C

Non glielo dia, perderà anche questo. Le dica che non è altro che un marrone marcio. Gli renda quel che gli deve. Prenda quelle armi, ma non le usi, le metta li. Marco e Luigia si mettono li, io mi metto qui. I giallo-rossi perdono ancora. È un banco di un mettro e è marrone. Il sole la rende gialla. Usa solo armi bianche, ma le usa da maestro.

Tabelle 1 & 2

Frasi di tipo A

Come, mi dà quel che è mio? Di chi è questo? Il vostro è lí sotto. Non ho che lei. È chiaro sopra e scuro sotto. Abbiamo quello che abbiamo. Mi coglie rose rosse e gialle. Da lui non ci sto. Questo mi piace piú de quello. Il chiaroscuro non è un colore. Non è solo oro quello che riluce. Il mio è piú o meno come il suo. Se è verde, vive. Non lo ammetta. La nostra è a colori. I miei sono via. Ma che ha? Dove sono i Suoi?

Frasi di tipo B

Anch'io sono sottosopra. Sono piú chiara di lui. L'ha detto lí per lí. Ha un che di strano. Qui sotto c'è qualcosa. Meno male che è qui. Non ci vede chiaro. Sono allo scuro di questo. Era scuro in viso. Apre gli scuri. C'è chi è colto e chi non lo è. Sta sul chi vive. Non si sottometta al suo rancore. Lo vende sottobanco. È tale quale suo nonno. Abito sotto a voi. Abbiamo quanto ci basta. In quanto a me! Meno una vita modesta. Pendo dalle sue labbra.

Frasi di tipo C

Noto che ne avete piú di quanto ne volete. Gli amici dei suoi amici sono miei amici. Glielo dia a nome mio, altrimenti non lo prenderà. Hanno dedicato la loro vita all'amore. Ne abbiamo chiarite di cose, anche quando non era nostro dovere! Metta in chiaro quello che ha da dire. Alla luce del sole ha gli occhi del color del mare, al chiaro di luna li ha neri. Che diritto ho io di giudicare i loro amici? So quali sono i miei doveri e i miei diritti.

Tabelle 1, 2 & 3

Frasi di tipo A

Prima o poi è lo stesso. L'ho chiamato a lungo. Va indietro? Lei è piccola piccola, lui grande grande. Ci ho messo un'ora. Per me non è suo. L'ho atteso a lungo. Per chi mi prende. Va a piedi. È una gran cosa. Il piú piccolo ha due anni. Mi dia una mano. Questa è roba di scarto. Le ha promesso il mondo. Non glielo permetta. E poi? Da piccolo avevo gli occhi blu. È cosí sottomesso. Da adesso in poi non lo chiamo piú. Li ha messi uno contro l'altro. L'ha preso adesso adesso. Macché! Si sottintende. Tra questo è quello non c'e differenza. Ha preso piede. Ha il viso pieno. È pieno di errori. Si metta a sinistra. Vanno uno dietro all'altro. Non è difficile chiamarci. L'ho ingrandito.

Frasi di tipo B

Sono alla mano. Lo metta nero su bianco. È pieno di sé. Mi sta tra i piedi. Lo guarda in lungo e in largo. La sinistra è rossa. Nel suo piccolo sa quello che fa. Si tolga dai piedi. Si da un gran da fare. Mi sono dato per malato. Non ci ho visto piú. Mi tolga questo peso dal cuore. Si fa mettere sotto ai piedi. Non me l'ha data a bere. Una mano lava l'altra. Se ne lava le mani. Non è un granché. Il senno di poi. L'ha sorpreso sul fatto. Li ho trovati con le mani nel sacco. Hanno fatta man bassa. Si è instradato lo stesso. Davanti a questo mi ci tolgo il cappello. Una cosa tira l'altra. Hanno perso piede. L'hanno messo in opera.

Frasi di tipo C

Luigi le va dietro, la chiama, la richiama ma lei va per la sua strada e non si ferma. Lo amo piu di ogni altra cosa al mondo. Olga non gli ha permesso di prenderle la mano. Vedo che questa cosa va per le lunghe. Si renda conto che su lui, non ci conto piú. Lo ha preso per il naso, ma lui non ci fa caso. È chiaro che questo deve restare tra noi. Premetta che è un ordine del re. Non si merita di chiamarsi mio amico, e io non lo chiamo tale.

Tabelle 1-4

Frasi di tipo A

L'ho detto a pochi. Non mi ha dato molto. Vanno e vengono. Per quanto ci capisco io non è essenziale. Dice, dice ma poi non fa niente. Per favore vadano uno per uno. È compreso nel prezzo. Ci vanno in pochi. Io non gliel'ho detto. È ancora troppo piccolo per questo. Lo porti dal medico. Me l'hanno portato già. Non finisce mai. È finto? Non gliel'ho detto io! L'ha ricostruito da solo. Prima di andare, ringrazialo. Si costruisce una scala a pioli. Parlano tra loro. Se da sei toglie due, resta quattro. Parla tra sé a sé. È uno studente molto istruito. Li punisce senza pietà. Mi parla ancora? Non è ancora finito. L'ancora non è ancora abbassata. Quello che ho fatto l'ho fatto invano. Ha grande riguardo per lui.

Frasi di tipo B

Non la finisce piú. A me questo non dice molto. Viene di quando in quando. È molto compreso di quello che fa. Lasciami in pace. Questo non mi va giú. È grande e grosso e ancora non lo sa fare.

Già, cosí se la prende lei, eh! Stravede per lui. È caduto in basso. Si metta in guardia, è pericoloso. È un basso meraviglioso. I grandi sono di sopra. Non si è fatto vedere. Studia come una matta. L'ha detta grossa. Si toglie il pane dalla bocca per loro. Ho molta fame, ma non ho sete. Non ci fare caso, straparla. Cosa fatta, capo ha. Grazie a Dio, è finito. Perche parli a vanvera? A detta dello studente non è ancora costruito. Si riguardi. Quello che è fatto è fatto.

Frasi di tipo C

Rossa in viso, gli ha dato la mano senza guardarlo negli occhi. La costruzione va per le lunghe; se non finisce prima che arrivi, poveri noi! Apra quella scatola e guardi cosa c'è dentro. Siamo indifferenti alle sue grazie ma ne siamo consapevoli. Mi ferisce quando mi dice che non valgo un fico secco. Quello studente è sul vano della porta, in piedi, e recita poesie liriche giapponesi. Cala l'ancora qui ché il mare non è alto. Abbassa la voce per favore, dorme ancora. È molto sofferente e giace supino sul suo letto, con lo sguardo fisso, senza dire una parola.

Tabelle 1-5

Frasi di tipo A

Non ne sa piú niente di nessuno. Sú, muovetevi. È tutta una scusa. Hanno rapito un uomo e una donna. Non le viene in mente niente? Venne via stravolta. Vadano due alla volta. Vada via. Fallo un poco alla volta. Quella è una vera donna. Vieni giú. Ci capisce? Non capisco niente. Si commuove per niente. Si tenga forte. Si adagi sul letto e non si muova. Parli piú piano, per favore. Quell'uomo viene da Roma. Quella donna e quel ragazzo hanno qualcosa in comune. Te li dò di volta in volta. Non mi viene nessuna idea. So tutto di lui. Tiene i soldi in banca. Che ne so io? È tutto un mondo.

Frasi di tipo B

Lui vede tutto nero, lei tutto rosa, ma nessuno dei due vede le cose per quelle che sono. Non sa di niente. Mi sa che non sa niente. Si adagia sugli allori. Gli ha dato di volta il cervello. A me non ha detto niente di niente. Non è nessuno. Sono diventata qualcuno. Tra me e lui non c'è niente. Eppur si muove. Questa volta è caduto in piedi. C'e un gran via vai. E tutto dire. È perfetto, non c'è niente da dire! Si tenga sú. Si comporti da uomo. Viene come viene. Lasciati andare! A poco a poco si sistema tutto. Per me e tutto. Non ci teniamo dalle risa. Tenga la destra. A questo ci tengo molto, non lo tocchi. Lo tengono in poco conto. Fanno i conti senza l'oste. Non si tiene piú dalla gioia.

Frasi di tipo C

Non tutto il male viene per nuocere. Comincio a capire perché quell'uomo non costrui la sua casa sul mare. Quella donna non sapeva come fare per parlargli, poi si è fatta forza e gli ha parlato. Quel ragazzo continua a dire che quell'uomo è suo padre; ma l'uomo lo nega. Sa suonare il piano con grande maestria. Prende qualcosa da mangiare? No, grazie adesso non mi va. Si comporti da uomo e la smetta di sparlare di tutti. Non c'è da fidarsi troppo di chi dice che si comporta solo da forte. Quel gatto randagio mi fa pena. Non le parli piú cosí, non vede che si commuove per niente? Con quella donna non c'è molto da fare; non la smuove neanche un masso.

Tabelle 1-6

Frasi di tipo A

Non faccio a tempo. Non lo trovo, non è al suo posto. Un posto per ogni cosa, una cosa al suo posto. Lo fa apposta. Mi guardi dritto negli occhi. Non ha ancora un posto. Il costo della vita è molto alto. Non ha fatto danno. Ho attraversato quella strada mille volte. Lo riconosco dalla parlata. Mi ha imposto di dire questo. Riconosco che non ne ho il diritto. Il mio posto a tavola è questo. Mi faccia sapere. Va dritto per la sua strada. Cerca di venire il prima possibile. Si unisca a noi. Mi unisco a voi. Quell'uomo è tutto curvo. È vero anche l'inverso. Sia gentile, stia ancora un pò di tempo. Sapevano chi era ma non lo conoscevano. È tardi, ma non sono in ritardo. Le impongo il silenzio. Il silenzio è d'oro. Striscia come un serpe. Si chiede se ne vale le pena. Non lo sapevo, l'ho saputo ieri da lei.

Frasi di tipo B

Venite a trovarmi. Mi è andato di traverso. Non guarda in faccia nessuno. Chi cerca, trova. Non si preoccupi per lui, ormai è a posto. Le hanno fatto largo. Se non è vero, è ben trovato. Tienti stretto a me. Conosco i miei polli. Non vedo che ci trova in quell'uomo. È una donna ricercata. Gli chiese troppo. Non c'è stato verso di smuoverlo. Non fare la faccia storta. Mi faccia vedere che cosa sa fare. Stia al suo posto. Non si è mai curato di farmelo sapere. Cosa fatta capo ha. Non riconosce i suoi errori. C'è giunto per vie traverse. Non prendere di traverso quello che ho detto. Sai che hai la faccia tosta? È stata davvero una trovata.

Frasi di tipo C

È una donna di fiducia, la conosco da lungo tempo. Si adagiò sul letto e vi rimase immobile per molte ore. Quell'uomo ha molti anni sulle spalle ma continue ad essere sano e forte. Ho sentito qualcuno muoversi di là, ma non capisco che sia, dato che siamo tutti riuniti qui. Non ci si capiva niente da quello che avevano detto, ma poco a poco è diventato tutto chiaro. Gli ho detto chiaro e tondo che ne ho abbastanza di lui; non capisco perché continua a cercarmi. È necessario che sia forte e stia assolutamente ferma se non desidera che le si faccia del male. È tardi, se non vado subito arriverò in ritardo. Mi confermi che il posto c'è, ed è per me. Stia attenta a quella curva, è pericolosa.

Tabelle 1-7

Frasi di tipo A

Non lo finisco per un insieme di cose. Chi vivrà, vedrà. È un uomo finito. Bene o male è finito. Il peggio non è ancora arrivato. Verrà, vedrà, vincerà. Nell'infinito c'è tutto. Da grande farà il pianista. Non mi sento né bene né male, ma sto meglio. È paro o dispari? È piuttosto stretto, ma non abbastanza. Quel libro e cosí leggero che lo leggerò velocemente. L'unione fa la forza. Lei è il mio solo bene. Gli pesa molto sulla coscienza. Ha il passo pesante e si vede da lontano. Sarà quel che sarà. Non sarà mica già cominciato? La legge dice cosí e non c'è niente da fare. Una cosa ben fatta e meglio di una cosa ben detta.

Frasi di tipo B

L'hanno fatto su larga scala. Detto fatto, se lo portò via. È un peso morto, e meglio gettarlo via subito. Prima di prenderlo, l'ha guardato in lungo e in largo. È un leggerone, non gli dia retta. Chi ben comincia, è alla meta dell'opera. Non lo sopporto piú, e cosí pesante. Parlano male di tutti. Il peggio è per lui. È un bel pezzo di ragazzo. Gli va male tutto. Va di bene in meglio. Cosí impari! Gesto di mano, gesto di villano. Se non ti sta bene, ben ti sta! Sta bene? L'ha detto cosí tanto per dire. L'ha finito a mala pena. Ti fa male? Ha la mano leggera. Ha fatto male a non andare. Questo non fa male. Quel ragazzo è davvero un pezzo di legno. E un gran peso per me. Bene o male, è fatto. Mi va bene. Io me ne sto alla larga quell'uomo. Non andare al largo.

Frasi di tipo C

Quella mano è cosí ben fatta, che nessuno si rende conto che è di legno. Sono stati insieme per anni, poi si sono separati senza rancore. Stanno sempre insieme, ma non sono affato uniti. Parla molto lentamente e si fa una gran fatica a capirla. E piuttosto pesante, ma è veloce come il vento. Hanno cominciato male e hanno finito ancora peggio. È molto generoso e spende largamente tranne quando qualcuno glielo chiede. È meglio se non legge quell'articolo di legge ad alto voce.

Tabelle 1-8

Frasi di tipo A

Leggono uno di fronte all'altro. Spesso mi rispondeva quando lo chiamavo. Non vuole mai andare a spasso. E davvero bello. Ha letto e letto ma non ha imparato niente. Perché va sempre di fretta? Dovete scrivere di piú se volete diventare scrittori. Sta a letto perché non sta bene. Non lo trovo, ma guarderó meglio. È brutto come il diavolo. Mangia spesso fuori? Ora è fuori pericolo. E bella come un angelo. Ma se è appena venuto! Dovete rispondere alla legge. Ci vuole molto tempo per farlo bene. È un modo di parlare prettamente studentesco. Quello che dice non risponde al vero. Che vuol dire? Avrà finito entro l'anno.

Frasi di tipo B

È svelto di mano, per questo è andato dentro. Mi vuole cosí. Viene spesso e volentieri. Mi hanno lasciato completamente fuori. Non me ne volere. È la donna che ci vuole per questa situazione. Li ha tagliati fuori. Va avanti sempre meglio. Ho voglia di molte cose. Risposero al fuoco con il fuoco. Non dire sempre cose fuori posto, per favore. Non si permetta di rispondermi. Abita in una strada fuori mano. Non l'ho mai visto cosí fuori di sé. Lo voglio piú che mai. Rispondo io di quel regazzo. Non si darà mai per vinto. Non vi dobbiamo niente. È al dentro della questione. O dentro o fuori. Io in questo non voglio entrarci. Che brutta faccia che hai! È un fuorilegge.

Frasi di tipo C

Non muore foglia che Dio non voglia. È meglio stare solo con le persone a cui si vuol bene. La tranquillità d'animo viene dal di dentro non dal di fuori. L'erba voglio non esiste neanche nel giardino del papa. Fuori non fa quasi mai bello, e non si vive bene senza sole. Spesso si parla senza sapere bene quello che si vuol dire. Nessuno è al di sopra della legge. Nel far fronte alle difficoltà, si è costretti a por mente a ciò che si fa. Il bello e il brutto non sono qualità assolute. Non ha fretta di parlarvi, vuole prima sapere di che opinione siete.

Tabelle 1-9

Frasi di tipo A

La leggerezza di quella donna è davvero straordinaria. Lo chiudo a chiave. Quel regazzo andrà all'estero. Ti sono vicina anche nella lontananza. È molto abile ma non è colto. Lo ha capito leggendo. Potevano chiedermelo. Si può camminare fino a lí e non oltre. Non allontanarti troppo. Penso che sia meglio se glielo dai tu. Vieni, avvicinati! Gli avranno già parlato! Pensaci su prima di rispondermi. Sebbene fosse molto veloce non ha risposto alle aspettative. Fa quel che può. Chiuda la radio. Se fosse facile non chiederei aiuto. Potevano pure dirmelo! Penso di andarci subito. Se fosse brutta, capirei! Essere o non essere questo è il dilemma.

Frasi di tipo B

Avrà un duecento anni! Hanno fatto lega. È roba fina. Quel ragazzo andrà lontano. Mi è capitata bella. È un uomo molto chiuso. Quasi, quasi, ci vado anch'io. Si è aperta con lei. Gli capita sempre qualcosa. Questa non ci voleva proprio. Non è niente, solo un pensiero. È un parente lontano. Mi è capitata tra capo e collo. La vuol capire che non voglio? Non prenderla troppo alla lontana, altrimenti nessuno capirà. Lontan dagli occhi lontan, dal cuore. Non le sono affatto vicino. Mi è oltremodo utile. Il mio vicino di casa è molto simpatico. Non ho potuto farci niente, mi hanno legato le mani. Questi concetti non legano. Non gli parla piú perche se l'è legata al dito. In questo caso io chiuderei un occhio. Non pensi piú a quella storia, ormai è una faccenda chiusa.

Frasi di tipo C

È difficile capire com'è nel suo vero essere. Non posso vedere quello uomo, è un essere insopporta-bile. Quando era lontano, ho capito di amarlo piú di ogni altro. Ha pensato lungamente e senza leggerezza a quello che gli hai detto. Sebbene capisse tutto e fosse aperto a ciò di cui si parlava, non aprì bocca. Non ci vedeva da lontano, cosí fu costretto a mettersi gli occhiali. Dischiuse le mani e l'insetto prigioniero fuggí. L'apertura è stretta e non si può passare se non si è abbastanza agili.

Tabelle 1-10

Frasi di tipo A

Ha imparato a scrivere presto. Uscite con me? Succeda quel che succeda, io esco. Non spero di vederla tanto presto. Le dissi di sí. Scelgono di fare quello che vogliono nella loro vita. Cosa succederebbe se tutti fossero come lui? Quel giovane non è il primo. È una vecchia storia. In gioventú scelse di andare lontano dai suoi. Lo ha trovato durante la vecchiaia. Te lo dissi perché tu capissi un pò. E fu subito sera. Inclina a pensare che e tutto un equivoco. Lo fece durante gli anni giovanili. Quel piano è inclinato. Venga all'ora esatta. Ha avuto grande successo. Quello che ha detto è inesatto. Malgrado sia vecchio è ancora molto agile. Come si scrive? Ce lo fece capire spiegandocelo con pazienza.

Frasi di tipo B

Non ne posso piú, mi esce dagli occhi. Non riesco a farci niente. La sa l'ultima? Chi è? Non so, uno nuovo. È portato alle scienze esatte. Disse l'ultima parola. Non sai quello che uscí dalla sua bocca! Non ha inclinazione per la musica. Entrerà o non entrerà? Sono l'ultima ruota del carro. Non posso mettere questo vestito, non c'entro! Chi tardi arriva, male alloggia. Tacete che siete gli ultimi arrivati! Quel posto significa la sicurezza. Fate pure! In questa faccenda non ci vuole entrare. Mi è uscito di mente. Di dove sono usciti quei due? Questa rivista esce spesso. Non gli è ancora entrato in testa? Lo metta per iscritto.

Frasi di tipo C

Non si può scegliere se non si sa quello che si vuole. È meglio imparare da giovani che il successo nel mondo non e una cosa importante. Chi lascia la strada vecchia per la nuova non sempre male si ritrova. Durante questi ultimi anni il mondo è diventato piccolo. Qualcuno disse che chi va piano va sano e va lontano e chi va forte va incontro alla morte. Tutti i vecchi sono stati giovani una volta, ma non tutti i giovani saranno vecchi. Molti uomini si chiedono il significato della vita, pochi lo trovano. Si può scegliere di sperare, ma non tutti sanno che è una scelta che si può fare.

Tabelle 1-11

Frasi di tipo A

Qualunque persona può chiamarlo. Lo metta lí, contro il muro. Lo ha guardato attentamente, ma non ha visto molto. È tanto distratto che non lo si può lasciar guidare. Ognuno fa quello che può, o quello che vuole. Le piacerebbe andare in giro per il mondo? Il cambio non e favorevole di questi tempi. Se non foste tanto distratti potrei fidarmi di piú de voi. C'è andato comunque. Facciamo a cambio? Ho molto freddo anche se non fa freddo affatto. Mi piace caldo. Se ne hai bisogno, bisogna andarlo a prendere. Manca poco alla fine. Mi serve proprio quello che manca. Siccome era rotondo, l'ho dovuto cambiare. Invece di guardarmi, parla! Fa proprio freddo!

Frasi di tipo B

È una persona quadrata. Mi faccia il santo piacere di tacere. Finí come a Dio piacque. Ha fatto parte di quella tavola rotonda. Andiamo alla tavola calda? È un uomo qualunque. Uno contro tutti. Questo pero è vecchio, però fa delle pere buonissime. Si è distratto ed è caduto. Il dado è tratto. Che ti manca nella vita? Abbiamo fatto cifra tonda. Ogni tanto bisogna distrarsi. Mi dispiace ma quell'uomo io non lo tratto. È il ritratto di suo padre. Ha contratto il tifo. Va a destra e a manca. Hanno mancato il colpo. Scusami se ho mancato. Non è mai stato un qualunquista. Lo ha ricevuta freddamente. Gli manca sempre la terra sotto i piedi. Glielo dissi chiaro e tondo. È un mese tondo che è partito. Tutto questo lo lasciò freddo. Piangere non serve. Pianse a calde lacrime. Il brutto è che lo fece a sangue freddo. Ha le spalle quadrate. Dica pure: a me non fa né caldo né freddo. È meglio non discuterci, ha la testa calda. Non si serve abbastanza della propria testa. All'improvviso gli mancarono le forze.

Frasi di tipo C

A tutti piacerebbe essere sempre attenti e presenti a sé stessi, ma spesso si è distratti e con la testa sulle nuvole. Fa freddo quando non c'é il sole ma quando esce, fa caldo e si sta bene. Invece di chiedere sempre aiuto perché non cominci a servirti delle tue risorse! Non mi sembra che ti manchi niente per essere padrone della tua vita. A me piacciono i fiori, però a quelli che mi hai portato ieri mancava qualunque profumo. Quando ebbe quell'incidente venne a mancare più volte e sembrava che nessun aiuto servisse a rianimarla. Venga pure in qualunque momento purché non sia troppo tardi.

Fu un incontro molto freddo: ognuno sperava che l'altro facesse il primo passo. Siccome nessuno dei due lo fece, tutti e due rimasero lí, senza sapere che dirsi; e invece di capire la propria timidezza ognuno dette la colpa all'altro per la mancata riuscita dell'incontro. Comunque sia, un primo incontro c'è stato.

Tabelle 1-12

Frasi di tipo A

Cosa porterà il futuro? Il presente non esiste; c'è solo il passato e il futuro. Domani è un altro giorno. L'autunno è la stagione che piace alle persone sentimentali. Non posso prevedere il futuro. Mercoledi mattina avrò bisogno di lui. D'inverno la notte e piú lunga del giorno. Siamo già a luglio? No, la prossima settimana. Aprile non ti scoprire, maggio vacci adagio. Ama il tuo prossimo. Abbiamo passato un lungo pomeriggio insieme. A domani! Ho passato una brutta notte. Non ero presente quando mi ha chiamato. Parto durante la bassa stagione. È di legno stagionato. Ci vediamo stasera all'angolo della strada. È alle prime armi. Beati gli anni verdi! La presente situazione politica è molto grave.

Frasi di tipo B

Una rondine non fa primavera. È illuminato a giorno. Vive giorno per giorno. Conosce tutti i fatti del giorno. Oggi giorno tutto può succedere. Roma non fu fatta in un giorno. Queste mancanze sono all'ordine del giorno. La notte porta consiglio. Peggio che andar di notte. Lavoro alla giornata. Ha finito i suoi giorni tutto solo. È arrivato a notte alta. Ha fatto le ore piccole. Non è mai presente a sé stesso. Mi ha fatto presente che tutto era cambiato. Mi tenga presente se c'è un lavoro. Era notte fonda quando una ladra rubò tutto. È uno scapolo stagionato. Fece di notte giorno. È fuori stagione. È stata una brutta annata. È passata quella stagione della vita in cui il futuro è sempre presente. Durante la stagione morta in questa citta non c'è vita. Sta sempre in mezzo come mercoledí. Che giornata! Parte giovedí notte.

Frasi di tipo C

Quando l'ho visto era molto stanco, ha detto che era un mese che passava ogni notte in bianco. Quando si è alzato stamattina mancavano dieci minuti alle otto, ma fuori era ancora notte perché è ancora inverno.

Le stagioni sono cambiate: a febbraio non ha fatto tanto freddo, ma a oprile fa un freddo cane. Sembra che si possa contare solo sui mesi estivi. A giugno e luglio sicuramente farà un gran caldo.

Lavora dalla mattina alla sera e di notte non riesce a chiudere occhio.

Mi sembra ieri che eravamo insieme e passavamo i mesi d'autunno in riva al mare a guardare e contemplare le navi che si allontanavano verso mondi sconosciuti. A quel tempo ci chiedevamo cosa ci avrebbe portato il futuro.

Spanish

Làmina 1

Ejemplos del tipo A

¡Tenla! ¿Ud. aquí? ¿Uds. también? ¡Tómelo! A mí no. A Ud. sí. Es verde. ¡Entre! ¡No entre! Ésa está entre las mías. Está solo. No tengo, sólo Ud. tiene. Ud., no él. No lo sé; lo sé. No me lo tomes, ¡es mía! Pon sólo una! No ponga ésas sino éstas. Si le doy ésto ¿qué me da Ud.? Ni a él se lo das ni a mí. La orilla de la làmina es blanca. Toma mi mano. Tómame de la mano. Dame la mano. Pos tus manos en las mías. Ésta está en tu mano. Métalas en la mano. De aquí a allí. ¡Siga! Siga tomándolas. Véalo. Mídalo.

Ejemplos del tipo B

Aquí y allí. ¿Qué tiene él? De una en una. Que entre solo. ¡Aquí no entran! Eso no entra ahí. La que sea. No las tengo ahí. Aquí me tienes. Me tiene a mí. ¡Qué tú lo digas! Es tarde. No es tarde, aún tiene tiempo. Dentro de un día; ¡Qué solo está! No está en sí. Aún está verde. No es azul sino azulado. ¿De veras? El sol se pone en la tarde. ¿Se pone Ud. roja? Póngase de pie. Póngase a pensar. Póngase entre ésta y ésa. Las medias se le caen. Ud. lo ama y él también a Ud. A Ud. le tocan las verdes y a él las rojas. Ud. póngase al lado de Tomás. Me quedan sólo tres. Eso no está a mano. Están mano a mano. En tus manos lo dejo. Me pongo en tus manos. Toma todo en serio. No te metas en esto. Se mete en líos . . . de ahí que tenga tantos. El está bien y tú también. El traje está a la medida. Tengo que verlo. ¡A ver, a ver!

Ejemplos del tipo C

La casa está en medio de la isla. A medio camino está la casa. Eso está a orillas del mar Rojo. Sólo sé que no lo sé. No me lo des a medias. Dáselo a solas, que no lo sepan. Aún a media luz lo veo bien. Lo tienen desde mediados del siglo. Me tocó en el alma su relato. Si te las dan bien, si no, bien también. Qué bien se está aquí! Tú me lo das y tú me lo quitas. Ud. se pone del lado de los rojos. Entre ésas me quedo con las azules. Lo deja sólo en la soledad de la tarde.

Làminas 1 Y 2

Ejemplos del tipo A

Tienes más que yo. Dale una más. No ponga más ahí. Ponga algunas más aquí. Es más corta que la suya. Eso es muy poco, déle más; El tiene mucho, Ud. nada. Éstas son tan pequeñas como ésas. ¿Cuántas tiene Ud.? ¿Cómo se llama él? ¿Son suyas? ¿De quién son éstas? Si no son suyas, ¿de quién son? Ésas son del mismo color; Estas son de otro color; ¿Cómo se llama la que está ahí? Nos dio unas pocas y se dejó las demás. ¡fuera de aquí! Ud. ponga una dentro. No tiene nada. No ponga ninguna. Esta blanca es nuestra. Pongámoslo entre tú y yo. Ya tengo muchas. Ud. Tiene muy pocas, tome algunas más. ¿Quién es? ¿Quién está ahí? No tengo nada más. Por aquí no están las rojas. El tiene una cosa pequeña en su mano. Tome una u otra.

Ejemplos del tipo B

¿Qué tal? Se puso más y más rojo. Las más grandes están demás, deja sólo las más pequeñas. ¡No más! Come a más no poder. Coloree esta lámina. Su pequeñez me asusta. Cuanto tiene lo da. Esta vez yo no lo tomo. Una vez sí, dos no. Véalo una y otra vez. Talvez ponga una roja en vez de una negra. Ud. es la que lo acortó. A cada uno lo suyo. Ni tanto ni tan poco. En cuanto a él . . . ¡Cuánto sol! De cuantos tiene el más grande es éste. Poco a poco ya tengo muchas. Por poco se caen. De a poco tienen todo lo que desean. Es tan así . . . Es tanto así, que . . . De nada. De ninguna manera. ¡Muy bien! Ni muy adentro ni muy afuera. Tal cual. No ponga allí nada más. Porque sí, Porque no. Nado poco.

Ejemplos del tipo C

¡Es tan grande el universo! Una vez tardó mucho en venir. Está demás que se opongan, de todos modos lo verá. Leer en colores es más entretenido. Una que otra vez tengo deseos de comer. Recorte un poco más de este lado, así quedará tan corto uno como el otro. Tomás es muy económico, no gasta en nada que esté demás. Tiene a su país muy dentro de sí. A muy pocos les llama sus amigos. Están afuera y tienen mucho calor; que se ponga el traje azul y la camisa color de rosa. Llamó un tal Tomás, no sé quién es, te llamará otra vez más tarde. Así lo maten no delatará a sus amigos. Amaos los unos a los otros como yo os amo.

Làminas 1, 2 Y 3

Ejemplos del tipo A

Tengo menos que aquel señor. Ésta es menos corta que aquélla. ¡Venga rápidamente! Ponga menos aquí que allí. Tiene cada vez menos. Quiere más de lo que tiene. Quiere tener todo para él solo. Quiero un poco. ¿Quién quiere el más grande? Estas dos no son del mismo color, estas otras sí. El más pequeño vale un peso. Tome cualquiera de ésas. El está cerca de aquí.

Ejemplos del tipo B

¡Gracias, muchas gracias! ¡Rápido! De nada. ¡Qué desgracia! ¡Hasta cuándo! Son tal para cual. El señor Verdi es muy gracioso. La señora era muy agraciada. Ud. tiene una mente muy rápida. Cuanto más tiene más quiere. Pon una verde, al menos. Pon por lo menos una verde. Déme muchas de éstas, a menos que no tenga bastantes. Él la echa mucho de menos. A ese señor lo tienen en menos. No vale la pena que lo devuelvas, sólo vale un peso. Quieras que no quieras, lo harás. Tómenlas al mismo tiempo. Lo mismo que Ud. yo estoy muy solo. Todo lo hace por sí mismo. Que se queden en su mismo puesto. Lo dejamos para otra vez. Dame una más paratenerdos. Tomás no para en casa. El tren no para en esta estación. ¡Listo! ¿Están listos para comer? ¡Si siquiera este carro fuera más rápido! Ni siquiera come bien. ¡Basta! Cualquiera que venga será devuelto a su casa. El tiene bastante más que Ud. Lo que Ud. tiene lo abastece a él. No te acerques mucho. Casi todos son mayores.

Ejemplos del tipo C

Nunca más lo llamará puesto que está muy lejos. De vez en cuando quiere alejarse un poco de los demás. Sólo quieren estar entre los suyos. El más pequeño vale un peso, el más grande dos, y el mediano uno y medio. Da casi todo lo que tiene y para sí mismo se deja muy poco; Para qué me da Ud. dos, sólo necesito una. El que está cerca de Tomás es José y el que está más lejos es Alejo. El acercamiento entre estos señores será muy rápido. A nadie le importa lo que Ud. piensa. No es ni más ni menos que un gran señor. Es un avaro, mientras más tiene más quiere. Su rapidez es lo que más admiramos. Aquello quedó muy lejos, después lo olvidamos. Casi toda la vida la pasó lejos de los suyos.

Làminas 1-4

Ejemplos del tipo A

La tomó mal y se le cayó. Ella come más que él. Es imposible venir cada día. Lo que ella dice es cierto. ¿Va Ud. al concierto? ¿Quiere algo? . . . ¿qué? Ponga algunas aquí, incluso una roja. Déme un buen poco de té. El día domingo es el mejor para mí. El mayor está lejos y el menor también. Con una más tendré doce; Desde aquí hasta ahí hay un metro. Sin ésas me quedan dos. Este señor es muy bajo. Póngase uno frente a otro. Espera hasta las dos solamente. Con esas dos ahora tengo trece. ¡Muy mal! ¡Muy bien!

Ejemplos del tipo B

Frente a frente. Tiene la frente grande. El caserón tiene quince metros de frente. Los soldados vuelven del frente. El país se enfrenta a un gran problema. ¡No es cierto! Fue un malentendido. Es un imposible. Es un acierto. Es un desacierto.

Su futuro es incierto. Ellas actúan de concierto. Por cierto, están todos de acuerdo. Algo es algo, peor es nada. Es un sinsentido. De día en día se le pasa la vida. Sus cuentas están al día. Está bajo ciertas condiciones. Junte todo lo que está por allí. No con quien naces sino con quien paces. La espera se hace desmasiado larga. ¡Abajo! Enuméralas de mayor a menor.

Ejemplos del tipo C

La casa tiene un ancho frente y está enfrente a un parque. Concertadamente se funciona mejor. Siempre nos dejan en la incertidumbre. Quiere el huevo con sal o sin sal, y el té, con azúcar o sin ella? La más bajita era una anciana muy graciosa, siempre que bajaba de la montaña se sentía muy bien. Desde lejos se veía la casa bajo los árboles. Ya sé que del dicho al hecho hay mucho trecho, pero . . . Desde lejos todo parece mejor. El señor Gómez dijo que era un asunto menor, pero en realidad, era de la mayor importancia. José mete la pata vez que dice algo. Dime con quien andas y te diré quien eres. Acerca de esto e incluso de eso discutiremos otro día. Pues como dicen: "a donde fueres haz lo que vieres," así hago yo.

Làminas 1-5

Ejemplos del tipo A

Dale los sesenta pesos. Cada día nos juntamos a las siete. Aquéllos vienen de cuatro en cuarto. Este es un cuarto más corto que aquél. Te espero a las seis. Entre cuatro y cinco estarán aqui. Ese trio canta bien. Déme sólo un cuarto de vino. Con una quinta parte estaremos contentos. Este senor es un millonario. Dame una docena de peras. No tengo ni la milésima parte de eso. Él vende por centenas. Son las tres y cuarto. Vienen por decenas. A quince la docena es muy conveniente. Ella tiene cerca de treinta y cinco. Aquel señor está medio dormido. Dio mil vueltas por el mismo lugar. Mil gracias. Un millón de gracias.

Ejemplos del tipo B

Es un ciempiés; Ella anda por los treinta. Lo puso de vuelta y media. Lo hace todo en un dos por tres. Sólo hay una entre mil como ella. Se lo dijo a media voz. Él tiene el tres de espadas. Se va siempre a medianoche. A mediodía el sol quema. Le dijo las mil y una. Tiene una millonada de cuentos siempre listos. Nos vamos a medias con las ganancias. A la una, a las dos, y a las . . . tres; Ya va por la cincuentena. No tengo un centavo. Ud. tiene el seis de oros y el ocho de copas. Es tan cierto como que dos y dos son cuatro. Como ése aquí los hay por miles. Me debe una quincena. No le busque las cinco patas al gato. Hay un tanto por ciento de comisión. Al cinco por ciento no está mal. Pesa como un quintal. Tenía las siete vidas del gato. En un quinquenio han hecho mucho. Lo dice a los cuatro vientos. No es nada de tonto, a vivo vivo y medio. No vayan uno por uno, vayan de a cuatro o cinco.

Ejemplos del tipo C

La aldea fue diezmada por los mosquitos. Ese es el monumento al centenario del país. No he pagado el diezmo. El pueblo estaba en cuarentena a causa de la epidemia. En cinco meses si lo he visto dos veces, es mucho. La señora reza su novena. El señor no quiere el cuarto trece, dale el catorce. De centavo en centavo ya tiene una fortuna. Cada vez que lo veo me cuenta un cuento de las mil y una noches. A los ochenta, el señor Gómez aún se mantiene muy cuerdo. Los inmigrantes venian por cientos. Tráeme dos docenas de tomates grandes. Van a misa todos los días en cuaresma. Por más que quieras no puedes partirte en dos.

Làminas 1-6

Ejemplos del tipo A

Ven pronto. Ud. entre pronto. Quizás venga dentro de un momento. Tome la caja con la mano izquierda. Faltan tres rojas, devuélvamelas. Todavia tengo una azul. Tú estás antes que él. Vaya a su casa despacio. Ese tren es muy lento. El señor Gómez camina lentamente. José hace dibujos pequeños. Tome todas estas cosas y póngalas en diferentes lugares. Voy a comer un poco de pan. Voy a tu casa pronto. Mientras yo tomo éstas, tú toma aquéllas. Además de las rojas tengo las negras. Ambas señoras se parecen mucho. Deme dos, ambas del mismo color.

Ejemplos del tipo B

¡Hasta pronto! Ud. tiene que estar listo pronto. Quizás me dé lo que quiero. Desde antes que ellos estoy yo. A mi izquierda no hay nadie. Estoy mucho más a la izquierda que a la derecha. Hace falta un buen bajo en el coro. Hace mucho que vivo aquí;. Por lo menos hace un mes que no lo veo. No faltaba más, yo lo haré. Si te doy doce de las que tengo, todavía me quedan muchas. Para encontrar la salida vaya por la derecha. No vienen todavía, talvez más tarde. No es una mala persona, antes es muy bueno. Despacio pasa el tiempo cuando se es muy joven. Hace calor. Ella hace lo que le da la gana. Estas dos son pequeñas y por lo tanto pueden estar en un espacio tambien pequéno. Después de eso todo puede ser. Él ve todo en cámara lenta.

Ejemplos del tipo C

En la mano izquierda tengo algo diferente de lo que tengo en la mano derecha. Su falta no se puede perdonar asi como así. José es lento pero capaz. Tomás y José son muy buenos, ambos están siempre listos para cooperar. Quizás Tomás venga cuando sepa que hemos encontrado sus siete mil pesos. Hacía mucho frío, tanto que no pudimos hacer partir el coche. Le faltaba muy poco tiempo para encuentra la veta de la mina cuando los otros lo hicieron. De pronto los días se vuelven más largos y uno encuentra que el sol no calienta. Faltan todavía algunos meses para que el estudio esté completo. Mientras más áspera es la senda por la que andamos más larga se la siente. Hacia donde él vaya irán los demás. Ninguno puede faltar a tan importante reunión a menos que sea por un asunto de fuerza mayor. Después de los años mil vuelven las aguas por donde solían ir.

Làminas 1-7

Ejemplos del tipo A

Pon éstas encima de ésas, es muy fácil. Blanco y azul son colores distintos. Este señor viene cada día a distinta hora. Ella se puso un vestido nuevo. Estas amarillas son iguales. Termínate toda la comida! Pon ésta al final de la linea. Vaya tras José, sígalo. José va primero, después lo sigue Tomás. Estas seis verdes se parecen aunque una es más oscura. Primero tome las más grandes, después las más pequeñas y por último las medianas. Ponga todas las más altas separadas de las más bajas. Sepárense en dos grupos. Este cuento no tiene fin. Alguien llama a la puerta. Esos dos se parecen mucho. El viejo siguió por la derecha y el joven por la izquierda. Ya se acaba el tiempo, hay que terminar.

Ejemplos del tipo B

¡Se acabó! Sé que no está, pero por si acaso, llámalo. ¿Qué le parece la opinión del señor Gómez? Lo que ellos dicen es cierto. Dice muchas cosas con facilidad. De nuevo viene aquel señor tan raro. Se tratan de igual a igual. Quieren igualarse en todo a sus vecinos. Al igual que tú él está solo. En fin, ya está hecho. ¡Por fin viene! Es un asunto sin fin. Se mete en un sinfin de asuntos. Mientras tanto la vida sigue su curso. Parece que va a nevar. Me parece que no tienen lo que dicen. En último término lo harán como sea. Están separados desde hace dos meses. Dice que lo terminó, sin embargo no me consta. Ellos tienen tiempo para todo. Puede ser que Ud. lo encuentre dificil, sin embargo a poco de empezar lo encontrará muy fácil.

Ejemplos del tipo C

Decirlo es fácil, hacerlo es dificil. No siempre es fácil encontrar lo que está delante de nuestras narices; Aunque sé que no tienes como devolverme este dinero te lo facilitaré. Aunque es más alto y tiene las piernas mucho más largas, anda mucho más despacio que José. Al fin y al cabo hace siempre lo que quiere. Por fin tiene lo que tanto quería, por supuesto que le costó bastante conseguirlo. José empiece a las seis a fin de que termine a las ocho. Nadie lo tiene, pero alguien tiene que tenerlo. Ponga primero la más pequeña y después la más grande . . . ya sé que es dificil, pero puede hacerse. Los últimos que vinieron no encontraron nada. Adelántense los que sean mayores de edad. Así es la vida, fueron muy ricos, sin embargo ahora no tienen nada.

Làminas 1-8

Ejemplos del tipo A

¡Saiga de aquí! ¿Escribe Ud. poesía? Tomás vende su coche en tres mil pesos, ¿quieres comprarlo? Suba al segundo piso. Ponga una cantidad igual en cada caja. Conteste a mi pregunta, por favor. ¡Contesten rápidamente! Ese señor habla solo. Ese traje por seiscientos pesos es muy caro. Ponga una sobre la mesa pequeña y una sobre la grande. Si le sobran algunas, démelas. En el próximo tren llega Luis. Ese edificio tiene varios pisos. La ventana está abierta. Busca dos azules, si las encuentras, dáselas a Juan. Cuatro es el doble de dos. Escribí tres cuartetos. No compro de lo más barato. Nos demoramos una hora desde la casa hasta aquí.

Ejemplos del tipo B

El tren sale a las ocho en punto. Así no sale bien, ensayen otra vez. este lápiz no escribe, hay que sacarle punta. Escríbale a su tía más seguido. Te lo dije: "es un vendido." Luis vendió su coche. El señor Rojas es un vendedor viajero. El agua subía de nivel en el lago. Me pisaron un pie en el metro, todavía me duele. No quiero sus sobras. El tren se aproxima lentamente. Aproximadamente son veinte. Este muchacho aprende casi todo de inmediato. El color de las hojas varia según la época. Por causas muy variadas están ellos aquí. Están tan abiertos al diálogo como nosotros. Pepe tiene un doble, cuando están juntos nadie sabe cuál es cuál. No hay demora, enseguida sale el tren.

Ejemplos del tipo C

Salgo de viaje dentro de un mes. Allí venden mucho más barato que aquí. Todo está cada día más caro, los precios suben sin medida. José sube rápidamente porque es un ambicioso. No es la cantidad sino la calidad lo que apreciamos. Se le cayó un peso y lo pisó sin darse cuenta. Vinieron varias señores a preguntar por las varios razones de la demora. Lo barato cuesta caro por eso nunca compro lo que parece menos caro. Juan compra vino en cantidades industriales y sólo bebe él en toda la familia. Lola no quiere dar su sitio a otro antes de tener un nuevo puesto pues dice que más vale un pájaro en la mano que cien volando.

Làminas 1-9

Ejemplos del tipo A

Su nombre es Diego. El color verde claro me parece mejor para tí. El tren no ha pasado todavía, pasa a las seis. En esta caja caben solamente diez, ¿cuántas caben en aquélla? Este traje ya no me cabe. Traje todo lo que me llevé el otro día. Vacie todo lo que haya en la caja. Ahora la caja está vacia. Óyeme aunque sea sólo por un minuto. El color verde obscuro le queda muy bien. Llevemos las rojas al cuarto piso. Es suya, llévesela. Abramos las ventanas para que entre aire puro. Deja la puerta bien cerrada cuando salgas. Yo no lo recuerdo a Ud. Lo conozco mucho. Conozco bien este camino. La gente venía desde muy lejos. Todos están conformes con la respuesta.

Ejemplos del tipo B

¡Arriba! ¡Arriba las manos! ¡Manos arriba! ¡Conforme! Está claro, no tengo ninguna duda. Claro que no podemos creer todo lo que dicen. Pasado algún tiempo se encontraron de nuevo. Deme dos huevos pasados. Su pasado no me interesa. Cabe decir que . . . No me cabe duda de que . . . Se lo dirás en mi nombre. Pase lo que pase él sigue en su sitio. Cayó al vacío desde cincuenta metros. Ya está muy obscuro. ¡Qué obscuridad! Lleva algún tiempo en ese mismo sitio. Acabo de llevarme un susto. Vive lleno de deudas. Habla mucho y no dice nada. No es como tú crees sino todo lo contrario. no tengo apuro, por el contrario, me sobra el tiempo. Dentro de un rato estarán todos aquí. Hace mucho que lo conozco. Cada vez que abro la ventana el viento la cierra.

Ejemplos del tipo C

Después de tan larga demora caben unas cuantas preguntas. Al contrario de ellos, Uds. tienen muy en claro la totalidad del asunto. Toda la gente no se conforma con las mismas preguntas y quiere proponer nuevos temas. No creo que quepa todo eso en este sitio tan pequeño, pero si quieres probar, puedes hacerlo. Desde que lo vi la última vez no creo que haya encontrado la cantidad que quería, ni siquiera un cuarto de ella. Tomás vive en las afueras, vive muy bien, pasa lo más del tiempo leyendo, claro que también le gusta mucho pasear por el campo. Los buenos recuerdos son gratos y nos encontramos gustosamente con ellos, pero los recuerdos ingratos tratamos de separarlos de nuestra memoria aunque casi siempre vuelven. Cuando la caja esté llena, todo lo que sobre póngalo en esta otra que, aunque diferente, es mucho más resistente y además tiene tapa. Si todos están conformes no puedo hacer nada.

Làminas 1-10

Ejemplos del tipo A

Hoy es lunes. Ayer fue domingo. Enero es un mes de treinta y un días. Venga temprano a las siete de la mañana. En las noches de invierno hace frío. Durante cinco minutos no tome sino de las más pequeñas. La semana tiene siete días. Cada dos semanas mamá va al cine. La mejor fecha para mí sería el tres de febrero. La primavera es la más hermosa estación del año. El día lunes ocho de agosto empieza el curso de español. El año tiene doce meses. Fue una buena tarde de verano. José paga sus deudas mensualmente. Durante toda la noche hizo calor.

Ejemplos del tipo B

Se obscurece temprano. A diario hacemos el mismo camino. Lola lleva un diario de vida. Este diario no trae la noticia. !Es tarde! El sol se pone al atarceder. Luis y María están de vacaciones. Al anochecer empiezan a salir las estrellas. Aquel día era miércoles de ceniza. Hasta la fecha no hemos sabido nada. Con fecha dos de abril vence su contrato. En el otoño de su vida aún luce muy joven. Vamos, se hace tarde. En abril aguas mil. Fue un día de semana santa. Luis pidió sus vacaciones adelantadas. Durante dieciseis años pagó el alquiler sin retraso. Diariamente compra sus provisiones.

Ejemplos del tipo C

De noche todos los gatos son negros. A pesar de su edad siempre tiene un aire primaveral. En invierno se obscurece más temprano. El diario de la mañana nos llega siempre con bastante retraso. En muchos países durante el invierno llueve y nieva mucho. No dejes para mañana lo que puedes hacer hoy. Mientras más tardemos en salir menos llegaremos. Ese señor salía a pasear a diario con su perro por el parque. Es un buen caminante, diariamente da un paseo de dos horas. Martes trece no te cases ni te embarques. Luis y María estaban de vacaciones cuando los vi por última vez. Durante muchos años pagó sus cuentas por adelantado y cuando no tuvo dinero ningún acreedor lo esperó. Hasta la fecha nadie ha hecho una cantidad tan grande como ella. Los deportes de invierno de la próxima temporada prometen ser todo un acontecimiento. Si Ud. se compromete a venir dejamos el quince como fecha final. El jueves santo era un día de mucha observación para las dos buenas señoras.

Làminas 1-12

Ejemplos del tipo A

El matrimonio Gómez tiene dos hijos. El hermano mayor se llama José. El hijo menor es Juan. González es un apellido muy común aquí. Tenemos muchos parientes. Hoy es tu cumpleaños. No conozco a ese primo. Hay siete personas en la sala. Sus antepasados eran de España. El marido de Juana no trabaja aquí. No sé cómo se llama la prima de Luis. Tomás tiene cuarenta años y aún está soltero. Juan es el yerno de los González. La nuera de don Simón es Lola. Es una familia numerosa.

Ejemplos del tipo B

Luis y Laura llevan diez años de casados. La abuela consiente a sus nietos. ¡Feliz cumpleaños! ¡Vivan los novios! ¡Qué parentela! Es una buena persona. Ese señor apadrina a los artistas. Lola está de novia con José. No recuerdo sus apellidos paterno ni materno. Los dos más pequeños son muy hermana-bles. José es muy buena persona. Luis es pariente cercano de José. Si Lila no se decide se quedará solterona. Tío y sobrino se entendían muy bien. Luis trajo la caja para que se la dieras a su novia.

Ejemplos del tipo C

Mi yerno Pedro es el marido de mi hija Rosa y mi yerno Luis es el marido de mi hija Laura. La buena señora habria comprado algo para su nieto si hubiera tenido dinero. La señora de Rojas celebra su santo y su cumpleaños. Lola dió la mayor fiesta de cumpleaños que se recuerda en el pueblo. Ella quería emparentarse con esa familia a toda costa. María no quiso casarse y eso que no le faltaban pretendientes. José tenia mucho de español por el lado paterno, pero por el lado materno mucho más de escocés. Cuando Luis era pequeño dejó de ver a sus parientes y sólo los volvió a encontrar después de veinte años. El buen señor no quería creerlo pues para un padre no hay hijo malo. La señora veía las faltas de su hijo can ojos de madre. Cada persona puede dar su parecer siempre que respete el de los de más. Hasta ayer nunca había visto a estos parientes. Cuando Ud. haya hablado con su hermano, llámeme para saber su decisión. Si vienes manaña no habré terminado aún, mejor ven pasadomañana. Dijo que no podía usar su coche, sin embargo lo acabo de ver en él. Luis nunca se comprometía con una posición determinada y eso no nos convenía. Considerando su pregunta fue que nos dimos cuenta de lo que se proponía.

Mandarin

表一：

红红绿绿	不深不浅	和颜	三色	没没
深深浅浅	不蓝不绿	浅浅	黄色	红颜
三三两两	不一一	他人	在在	人人
黑黑白白的	黑白的	白人	人们	三木
两把两把的	两、三人	红木	人儿	一把

— 有的人有，有的人没有。
— 他的人木木的
— 我们什么也没有。
— 他给我的是黑白的。
— 不拿白不拿。
— 他什么人也不是，我不给他
— 在这儿的人，黑黑的。
— 咖啡的颜色深深的。
— 我不拿也不给。

— 拿人！拿人！
— 放人！
— 什么人？
— 有你没我！
— 没什么，没什么！
— 你在拿什么？
— 人在是在，……
— 没有人色，白白的。
— 他的有没有这么红？

表一、表二：

端端正正	中间人	外行	一角	跟头
不上不下	木头人	左右	正直	正在
里里外外	个中人	中的	直角	平行
中黑外白	一下子	外人	人中	中外
上上下下	前人	中和	正面	和平
个个	后人	个人	面子	跟前
下人	正方	把子	儿子	橘子
中子	黑、白子	角子	一直	在

Appendices

— 跟着他！他到哪儿，你也到那儿。
— 外边儿黑黑的，什么人也有。
— 把"不"字和"正"字放在一起，成"歪"字。
— 他的儿子拿着橘子不放。
— 在他左右的人都是端端正正的。
— 在外交方面我们也都是外行人。
— 白人下黑子，黑人下白子。
— 三个角中有一个是直角。
— 他一下子站，一下子坐。
— 在上的人不正，在下的也不正。
— 那个白人的前后左右都是黑人，他一
— 个人站在正中间，面色白白的。
— 正面不平，另一面平平的。
— 他们的中间人，在这方面不在行，人也不正直。
— 都是深交，没有什么外人。
— 他们的中间人，在这方面不在行，人也不正直。
— 都是深交，没有什么外人。
— 这些橘子是他给我的，你们谁也不行拿。
— "白头人"是不是你的字！

— 哪里，哪里！
— 头大！关大！
— 不给不行。
— 没面子，没面子！
— 坐！坐！坐！
— 不成！不成！
— 着三不着两。
— 人人都有一个头。
— 躺一下。
— 把这个拿着。
— 木头人一个！

表一、表二、表三：

新旧交接	多方面	现成	再三	老成
新旧有别	有心人	直接	长子	空前
和而不同	浅薄	间接	同好	老子
空间	接头	老人	同行	高中
年关	矮子	胖子	人才	好人
同年	大人	空白	厚重	好色
老大	老三	两老	多端	大同

样子	和好	中空	别人	大有
大白	现行	现下	小人	同人
深长	中年	同心	不才	大成

— 他人很年轻，可是很老成。
— 老人现在大有起色，人长胖些，面色也好多了。
— 在大人面前，好好的坐着，不要没大没小的。
— 老三老是跟在老大左右。
— 站在那儿的那个人，又老又好色，不要跟他在一起。
— 那个大胖子年轻时，长得好高好瘦，和木条一样，直直的。
— 我一直都这么瘦，胖也胖不了多少。
— 你和我们的中间人接了头没有？
— 刚刚他好好的；可是一下子，面色成绿的了。
— 以前，好人在在；现在这个年头，没有什么好人了。
— 有时，他很浅薄，什么都要最新最大的，才拿。
— 起先，他们颜色深浅不一，大小也不一。现在都一样了。
— 他是老好人一个，给他什么都好。
— 小瘦子人小，面子大，人人都给他面子，他要什么给什么。
— 我和那个小矮子是一面之交，不是深交。
— 在上的人在时，在下的人都端端正正的；在上的人一不在，在下的人都不好了。
— 蓝高木有三个儿子；长子蓝大木，长得和他一样，高高大大的。中间的儿子是蓝中木，长得瘦瘦长长的。小儿子蓝三木，人很矮小，面色也老是白白的。
— "再三"和"一再"一样。
— 他胖时的样子，没有瘦时的好。

— 人之下，万人之上。	— 他小时了了	— 外重内轻
— 行行重行行。	— 老大不小。	— 不先不后
— 行将就木。	— 少年老成	— 好了！好了！
— 平起平坐	— 不了了之	

Appendices

表一、表二、表三、表四：

好好先生	七大八小	晚年	假期	天子
四面八方	七七八八	先天	分子	子午
十有八九	三头二面	后天	半子	重点
七长八短	三头两日	高明	期年	生字
月下老人	一日千里	天空	木星	生日
七上八下	七十二行	百行	白天	时差
三长两短	不三不四	四时	分红	明白
长生不老	千人一面	四下	早年	时日
长天大日	年深日久	起点	差别	百行

— 正月是一月。
— 3/7中，3是分子。
— 天上有很多星星。
— 中午最好，过早过晚都不太好。
— 过多过少都不行，这样多正好。
— 刚才我的咖啡明明在这儿；现在不在了，谁拿了？
— 万一他有个三长两短的，把这个给他儿子。
— 把这些小木头先点一点，再好好的刻一刻。
— 现在，人人都要上三年初中；高中，有的人上，有的人不上。
— 他生了儿子后，坐月子坐了两个半月。
— 我们坐过头了；在这儿下好了，差不了多少。
— "差一点儿"和"差不了多少"差不多。
— 他天生三三八八的，没有人要和他在一起。
— <u>小不点儿</u>天生才高，天下三百六十行，那一行都行。
— 半新半旧的那个比较重，也比较大。
— 在这儿，人人都是那个白头老人接生的；
大前天他过生日，年九十五，
我们给了他很多橘子和一个红木刻成的白头老人
。

— 过时不候！
— 他天生才子一个。
— 他人十分刻薄。
— 这个钟很好，一分也不差。
— 他们三三五五的躺着。

表一、表二、表三、表四、表五：

天高地厚	前因后果	方向	太空	自大
上天下地	去旧更新	太上	假期	深远
一差二错	大有可为	自白	一己	共同
天道好还	中人以上	大地	以太	一共
或多或少	三对六面	共和	太子	常人
来日方长	两可之间	对白	自传	太极
今是昨非	人一己百	行为	远大	外地
来去分明	别有天地	成人	是非	近来
自外生成	日就月将	去就之间	白头如新	

— 有生以来，没这么大方过。
— 有成就的人不都是天生才高者。
— 他对别人比对自己还大方。
— 为什么他老是在这儿转来转去。
— 离地越远，就越重。
— 对不起，我拿错了，还以为是我的呢！
— 太后去年就大去了，可是现在还在太平间里。
— 现在是非常时期，我们没有那么多，只有这些，
  你只好将就将就了；不要老是要这要那的。
— 要是每个人都先给后拿，或只给不拿，
  天下就太平了。
— 早晚都要去，还不如现在就去，
  人比较少，比较空点。
— 刚刚还好，可是一过三更，我的头越来越重，
  现在头里空空如也，什么都不行了。
— 以前，他非常自大浅薄，老是自以为是，
  以为自己什么都比别人好；现在好多了。
— 黄大使和他太太要的那个大木刻太重了，
  我自己一个人拿不来；
  明天我和几个年轻人接头后，
  要他们拿去，好不好？
— 可人的<u>白小红</u>老是若即若离，
  <u>蓝</u>先生黑头要成白头了。

— 你坐坐，我一下就来。
— 色即时空。
— 可一而不可再。
— 去你的！
— 行半里者半九十。
— 所为何来？
— 时不再来。

Appendices

表一、表二、表三、表四、表五、表六：

自然而然	日正当中	便当	反面	概论
生生不已	千了百当	连行	实行	当地
无时无地	反颜相向	由来	正当	无行
无可厚非	后来居上	必要	其他	必然
百无一长	天无二日	居所	相对	相好
以一当十	万夫不当	无我	如何	居间
直接了当	终其天年	反间	无上	宁可
若有若无	由己无人	了当	连坐	无须
大不为然	无因而至	居中	由于	自反

— 即使他要我上天下地，我也去。
— 今天他有点反常，怎么了？
— 他不管三七二十一就躺下去了。
— 上当了！这里头什么也没有，空空的。
— 人心不同，各如其面。
— 这儿是是非之地，要是不必要，你们还是少来吧。
— 方的那个又没有什么特别，
   你何必一定要那个呢？
— 这条对每个人以后都有方便，
   大概没有人反对吧！
— 去他那儿之前，须先经过白胖子哪儿，
   实在很不方便。
— 很多年轻人不管别人的反对，
   自由自在的同居起来了。
— 反正我们三个人是去定了；
   你们去不去，我也管不了了。
— 论才，他第一，无如其右者；论人，
   他最不老实；论相，他们几个人不相上下。
— 现在，她可望而不可即；可是，
   一而再，再而三，必有和她接近的一天。
— 他一生平平，没什么特别；小时了了，老大无成。
— 即使他们接二连三地来，也不过如此，没什么了不起。
— 他不但一无所长，而且好无中生有。

— 自由在何方？
— 从今后，何去何从？
— 反了！反了！
— 果然不错，太近了。
— 从头来！

表一、表二、表三、表四、表五、表六、表七：

前思后想	可想而知	大数	学长	浅见
头头是道	当行出色	大道	道行	开关
旧才新用	进而教之	告白	相关	才思
闻一知十	耳听八方	使用	告假	有关
应当之分	所见所闻	相应	喜爱	好吃
使之闻之	出于无意	接见	上学	上诉

— 我才一转，他就不见了。
— 给他点颜色看看。
— 管他的，先吃了再说。
— 知其不可为而为之。
— 百闻不如一见。
— 生而知之者，天才也。
— 他有出将入相之才，虽然现在仍没没无闻，
  以后定有出人头地的一天。
— 谁行为不好，不知自爱，就把谁开除。
— 说都说了，有用没用，只好听其自然了。
— 他有实才实学，用他做这个，
  不但大材小用，而且用非所学。
— 别多说了！你只知其一，不知其二，
  说了也是白说，没什么用。
— "听写"是先听再写。若一面听，
  一面写，可能会写错。
— 只要一看他的样子，
  谁都知道他是道道地地的好吃者。
— 他的爱人和他两地相思，
  吃不下也喝不下，现在好瘦。
— 他的用人爱说大话，其实及其不中用。
— 你们对我这么好，实在过意不去。
  这点小意思，请拿了吧！
— 白太太的儿子们，管教有方，
  有可爱又好学而肯上进。
— 意想不到！他看起来十分老实，
  居然只是说说而已。
— 千思万想以后，小白终于告诉我们她对小黑又意思。
— 那个红颜老人对他儿子们的所作所为，不相问闻。
— 他还年轻不知轻重，又无先见之明，
  所以到头来，什么也做不出来。
— 把前后一五一十地告诉我。
— 他能吃能喝，
  怎能不胖？
— 三思而后行？
  再思而行，可也！
— 你先来，请便，请便！
— 不敢当，不敢当！
— 一百星不如一月。

Appendices

表一、表二、表三、表四、表五、表六、表七、表八：

| 笑气 | 住所 | 忘八 | 空气 | 行走 | 叫卖 |
| 动向 | 笑颜 | 大指 | 推却 | 咬咬 | 呼应 |

— 真丢人！才跑这么一点，就上气不接下气，再也跑不动了。
— 昨晚一听了有关你们的新闻，我们就摸黑而来。
— 他从小就喜欢跟在大人后头，问长问短的。
— 买空卖空是极不正当的行为。
— 儿子们长大以后，一个个的都远走高飞，住在别地了。
— 我天不怕，地不怕，就怕和爱哭的人在一起。
— 不好了！不好了！他的呼吸停了，面无人色。
— 为了答谢你们的好意，我答应到他那儿，为你们说说好话。
— 明天早上七点正我们一起从这儿出动，过时不候！
— 有始有终，才能有所成就。
— 他面子好大，让我们左等右等，等了大半天，还不来。
— 在他跟前，我们都好怕，连大气也不敢呼一个。
— 不懂就问，别怕丢面子。不然以后，一多了，就更不明白了。
— 笑话！谁肯听他的。
— 那个买卖人才听了一半，就动气了，掉头而去。
— 那么小气的人和我们无关，我们从不相问闻。
— 答非所问，不如不答。
— 还没见面之前，他是何样人等，我们一望而知。
— 以上是我的一些意见，见笑大方了。
— 他们两人一唱一和，又叫又唱，一天一下子就过去了。
— 他已可非成是，再和他推论，也没用。太晚了！
— 大拍卖！大拍卖！不要错过这个天下第一大拍卖！进来看看我们有什么！你要买什么，我们有什么！拍卖！拍卖！

— ♪是四分之一拍的记号； 是半拍的记号；♩是一拍记号。
— 跟他推论了大半天，他还是无动于中。

表一、表二、表三、表四、表五、表六、表七、表八、表九：

会心不远	有一得一	总共	来往	先知后觉
万方多难	高下在心	指数	看穿	九死一生
心知其意	快意当前	大选	十全	千难万难

— 早知今日，悔不当初。
— 有借有还，再借不难。
— 万不得已，才请教于他。
— 三心二意，见一个爱一个。
— 他动不动就生气，很难相处。
— 他得过且过，一点也不知上进。
— 他们两小无猜，天生的一对。
— 要别人做，还不如自己来，快些。
— 随他去吧！心去难留，人大了，心也飞了。
— 那有什么了不起，等着看我的吧！
— 他十分心黑，只管自己好处，不管别人死活。
— 心平气和地和他说说，千万不要动气。
— 他说黑道白，连好好先生都被弄气了。
— 他说三不接两，弄得我们哭笑不得。
— 这个年头，做人真难，连做好人都得当心。
— 若没有重见天日之一日，不如一死了之。
— 他们被打得七死八活，真使人担心着急。
— 他随时随地为别人着想，真是难能可贵。
— 别多心了！他们管教有方，不会这么随便的。
— 知人知面不知心。
— 你太天真了，天下多的是黑心人；
　你真得十分小心。不然，上了当就悔不当初了。
— 无心之过，再所难免，
　看在我们是生死之交的面上，放了他吧。
— 他一哭，就哭得死去活来；
　可是，一笑，又笑得半死不活。
— 姓红的那小子，最近总是面有得色，
　不知又做了什么？

— 人在心不在。
— 人老心不老。
— 老死而不相往来
— 把他除了后人心大快。
— 两大之间难为小。
— 活该！谁要你不小心。
— 已忘了？真是贵人多忘！
— 老而不死！
— 往前走！
— 随便！
— 急死人了！
— 猜猜看！
— 到处都是人。
— 弄假成真了。
— 成全他们吧！
— 十分使人感动。
— 真象大白！
— 真是的！

Appendices

表一、表二、表三、表四、表五、表六、表七、表八、表九、表十：

一日三秋	雨虎	秋气	秋颜	中东	三国
鸡口牛后	国学	永夜	阴中	度数	国是
三冬二夏	阳春	暖和	西方	天国	木马
秋分点	国都	阴平	永生	近东	国定

— 天长地久，永不分离。
— 大地如春，万象更新。
— 一别如雨，何日再见？
— 一雨成秋，天凉多了。
— 一龙一蛇，各有所好。
— 不正经的人才天天买春。
— 每年的八月十五日是中秋。
— 深更半夜，他还是不停地呼叫。
— 西太后冷心冷面，从不把下人当人看。
— 两个儿子，一龙一猪，有如天地之别。
— 中国是远东国之一，是一个共和国。
— 他是东西南北人，没有一定的住处。
— 他别有会心，高人一等。
— 你要特别当心，他是笑面虎，居心不正。
— 两老终日终夜，做牛做马，还不是为了你们。
— 龙头蛇尾，不会有好果。
— 虎头蛇尾，长此以往，也不会有什么成就。
— 生大人的左右如蛇鼠横行，人见人怕。
— 久而久之，我们看穿了他的居心。
— 昨晚的"中国之夜"非常别开生面。
— 此地不但四季如春，当地人也很和气。
— 他一马当先，一往无前，直到被打死后才停。
— 平心而论，他们两人之才能，
　各有千秋，不分上下。
— 他指东话西，说了半天，
　真意是什么，就不得而知了。
— "下雨天，留客天。天留，我不留。
　下雨天，留客天。天留我不？留！"

— 把死马当活马看。
— 他傍若无人，大吃大喝。
— 雨过天晴，他们又和好如初。
— 当他的下人比猪狗还不如。
— "立刻"和"马上"意思一样。
— 此地，春无三日晴。
— "瘦猴子"不是好东西。
— 上西天了。
— 冷暖人自知。
— 蛇无头不行。
— 午夜是十二点正。

表一、表二、表三、表四、表五、表六、表七、表八、表九、表十、表十一：

部位	国本	百口	批点	片长	完本	套话
种别	次第	木本	张本	部居	本位	本色
架次	次比	本心	片方	全部	批答	次长

— 个子矮的人坐在前面。
— 弄口处有一卖包子的。
— 他是做进出口的。
— 他做错了，被打了一顿。
— 包太太本姓张，叫好学。
— 正本、副本各三份都在这儿。
— 他心直口快，有什么就说什么。
— 立场不正，再会说话也没用。
— 枝头上有一条白蛇，好怕人。
— 他打里打外，一天从早忙到晚，
　片刻不停。
— 有一个日本人，很会说双关话，
　听起来，很有意思。
— 明明要，可是口里偏又说不要，
　真是口是心非。
— 高空人架空而行，看得我们心跳口跳，
　坐也坐不住。
— 他块头大，气度小，和他打交道真使人头大。
— 打更的老人，几十年来，不论晴雨，天天都出现。
— 请把我的东西快打点一下，
　回头我就要走了；后天才回来。
— 先把方瓶口的都串在一起，
　再一个一个的把瓶口封好。
— 他不但总是心口如一，而且笑口常开，
　所以我们相处的很好。
— 别哭了；人已死了，再哭，再后悔，
　也不能使他起死回生。
— 很多年轻人，成双成对，在月下跳起来了，真动人。
— 浅薄者，一到外国就忘本了。
　只学会外国人的短处，而不知留住本国人的长处。
— 和小人和平共处，就等于和小人串通，没什么两样。
— 打坐不是一天一夜就可成；
　要从一而终，天天打，才有用。

— 各位先生，……
— 人得其位，位得其人。
— 如此十全者，天下无双。
— 空口说白话。
— 别东张西望！往前快走！
— 别听他的。他有口无心。
— 大地回春。
— 我们说了他一大顿，
　终于使他回心转意了。

Appendices

表一、表二、表三、表四、表五、表六、表七、表八、表九、表十、表十一、表十二：

表一	表二	表三	表四	表五
三男两女	千岁一时	祖上	岁夜	公论
三朋四友	天公地道	岁出	岁除	公所
通家之好	子子孙孙	中堂	朋分	国文
家人父子	日长岁久	如兄	妻亲	祖先
黑家白日	一男半女	学子	公转	子母
匹夫匹妇	爱亲做亲	外子	夫姓	家常

— 兄弟姊妹应相亲相爱。
— 大道之行也，天下为公。
— 公道自在人心。
— 有其父，必有其子。
— 男欢女爱，春色无边。
— 两姑之间，难为妇。
— 有如三日新妇，行动不便，度日如年。
— <u>牛小妹</u>极小家子气，没见过大场面。
— 今天我做东，请你们大家大吃一顿。
— 老死于祖国，是他一生最大的愿望。
— 公使常出公差，一年中有几个月不在家。
— 妻是人家的好！月是他国的圆！
— 他架子好大，非此不可，
  弄得大家不开心。
— 有家教的人不会随意借用别人的东西。
— 岁月如飞！一别就已二十多年了。
— "公平"，"公正"，
  "以公为公"是"偏心"的相反。
— 和那种三姑六婆打交道不会有好下场的。
— 公子哥儿，成天什么也不做，
  只是跟在女人后面打转。
— 她是高明妇人，相夫教子，极得公婆喜爱。
— 现下，在公共场所中，
  有不少红男绿女，亲亲热热，傍若无人。
— 妇女们，站起来吧！为我们的自由，而前进！

— 嫁鸡随鸡，嫁狗随狗。
— 男生、女生，分开坐！
— 难兄难弟，还分什么你我？
— 一国三公，何去何从？
— 有朋自远方来，……
— 行不得，也哥哥。
— 人人都应爱国。
— 老夫子有子弟三千。
— 一家之长，不好当！
— 非处女不婚！
— 一表人才，人见人爱。
— 她居然敢公然反对我们，
  胆大包天！
— 新婚夫妻，夫唱妇随；
  老夫老妻，不闻不问。

Bibliography

Caleb Gattegno 1   *Teaching Foreign Languages in Schools: The Silent Way.* First edition 1963, Educational Explorers Ltd., Reading England. — Second edition 1972 revised and with Appendices by Sue Wong, Jane Orton, Ghislaine Graf, Lolita Goldstein, Hilde Jaeckel, Cecilia Bartoli Perrault, James Karambelas, Maria del Carmen Gagliardo, Rosalyn Bennett and Robert L. Coe, Educations Solutions, Inc., New York, N.Y.

2   *Fidels* worked out for Arabic, Cantonese, Catalan, Cebuano, English, French, German, Greek, Haitian Creole, Hebrew, Hindi, Italian, Jamaican Creole, Japanese, Korean, Malay, Mandarin, Portuguese, Russian, Serbo-Croat, Spanish, Tagalog,

Thai, Turkish, Vietnamese. Printed only for English, French, Spanish also as *mini-Fidels*.

3 *Word Charts* for all languages above minus creole of Jamaica, Turkish and Vietnamese.

4 *Mini ESL* American Student *materials*. Specially devised in 1974 for use by students at home and in classrooms for independent studies.

5 *Video-tapes* in black and white mainly, both for teaching a language and for teacher education. For examination not yet for sale.

6 Articles, mainly in Educational Solutions Newsletter, Vol. 1, 1970 to Vol. V, 1976.

Earl Stevick 1 *A Riddle, with some hints for its solution* Action, Vol. 1 #10, Oct. 1973.

2 *Review article* on C. Gattegno 1. in Tesol Quarterly, Vol. 8, Sept. 1974.

Philippa Wehle *"J'enseigne le francais sans ouvrir la bouche"* Psychologie No. 78, Paris 1976.

Bibliography

Articles by Cecilia Bartoli, Clermonde Dominicé, Shiow Ley Kuo, James Karambelas, Patricia Perez and many others have appeared over the years in magazines and journals since 1970. See mainly Educational Solutions Newsletters.

www.ingramcontent.com/pod-product-compliance
Lightning Source LLC
Chambersburg PA
CBHW080536170426
43195CB00016B/2578